AN INTRODUCTION TO

Freud
and
Modern
Psychoanalysis

BY **HANS H. STRUPP**

Professor of Psychology
Vanderbilt University

BARRON'S EDUCATIONAL SERIES, INC.

Woodbury, New York

For Karen, Barbie, and John

PREFACE

Psychoanalysis as a theory of personality and method of psychotherapy is a topic in which people are always vitally interested. For one thing, it holds out the hope of understanding something about oneself and one's problems in living, of which everyone has his share. For another, it may help to fathom the feelings and motives of one's friends and associates. Closely related is the question of efficacy of psychoanalysis and related forms of psychotherapy, of which people avail themselves in ever increasing numbers. Part of this interest has been sparked by the growing public concern with problems of mental health as well as the emergence of other forms of psychotherapy, some of which are sharply opposed to therapy based on psychoanalytic principles. For these reasons, a short chapter dealing with these problems has been included.

My own interest in the area of psychoanalysis and psychotherapy has been chiefly as a student and researcher, secondly as a therapist and teacher. One can learn about psychoanalytic theory as one can learn about any other theory, that is, through one's intellect. However, a genuine understanding of the subject matter can only be acquired through one's experience as a patient. This fact was abundantly stressed by Freud, and it remains valid without question. Thus, to adapt one of Freud's metaphors, a book on psychoanalytic psychology can be no more satisfying in a deep sense than a printed menu can be a substitute for a meal. The most a menu can do is to whet one's appetite, and hopefully this little book will succeed in stimulating the reader to want to know more.

Finally, it is only fair to mention that, while I have striven to be objective, I am sympathetic to Freud's point of view. Although I recognize the gaps in our knowledge, I am deeply impressed with the originality, richness, and potential value of the theory. Like any good theory it raises more questions than it answers, but in my judgment it has' no serious contender.

NASHVILLE, TENNESSEE   *Hans H. Strupp*

ACKNOWLEDGMENTS

Thanks are due the following publishers who have generously authorized quotations from materials published by them:

Sigmund Freud Copyrights Ltd., Mr. James Strachey, and The Hogarth Press for permission to quote from *On the History of the Psychoanalytic Movement* (1914), *Lines of Advance in Psycho-Analytic Therapy* (1918), and *An Autobiographical Study* (1925), respectively in volumes 14, 17, and 20 of the Standard Edition of *The Complete Psychological Works of Sigmund Freud*. Additional permission for the American market was granted by W. W. Norton & Company: *An Autobiographical Study* (copyright 1935 and 1952) and *The Question of Lay Analysis* (copyright 1950). Similarly, a quotation from *On the History of the Psychoanalytic Movement* (Volume I of the *Collected Papers of Sigmund Freud;* Basic Books, Inc., Publisher, New York, 1959) was authorized by Basic Books, Inc.

Houghton Mifflin Company gave permission to quote from N. Cameron, *Personality Development and Psychopathology*, 1963.

Encounter (London, England) authorized a quotation from an article in the November, 1958 issue: G. Gorer, "Freud's Influence."

CONTENTS

As you know, we have never prided ourselves on the com-
pleteness and finality of our knowledge and capacity. We are just as
ready now as we were earlier to admit the imperfections of our
understanding, to learn new things and to alter our methods in any
way that can improve them.

Sigmund Freud (1918)
"Lines of Advance in Psycho-Analytic Therapy."
Standard Edition, vol. 17, p. 159.

CHAPTER 1

Freud's Life
and Work:
An Overview

The history of the major discoveries in psychoanalysis is largely interwoven with the life and professional carrer of a single man, Sigmund Freud. Within the confines of this book it is difficult to convey more than a hint of the man's tremendous productivity and the impact of his thinking on the development of psychology and psychiatry during the first half of the twentieth century. Nor has this influence been restricted to these specialized sciences; it has extended into literature, art, child-rearing, education, anthropology, philosophy — to name but a few. It is a commonplace that Freud has revolutionized the conception of the nature of man in modern times. It is equallly apparent that there are few men whose influence has been more pervasive and far-reaching.

Early Life

Sigmund Freud was born May 6, 1856, in Freiberg, a small town in Morovia, now in Czechoslovakia but at the time within the Austro-Hungarian Empire. His parents were Jews and he remained a Jew himself, although he had little interest in organized religion. His mother was twenty years old at the time of her marriage, and Sigmund was her first child, born one year later. Subsequently, five daughters and two other sons were born to the family, but Sigmund apparently was her favorite. In later years—she lived to the age of ninety-five—she referred to her famous son as *"mein goldener Sigi"* and Freud recorded the significant observation: "A man who has been the indisputable favorite of his mother keeps for life the feeling of a conqueror, that confidence of success that often induces real success." Ernest Jones, Freud's long-time associate and faithful biographer (see Suggestions for Further Reading), adds: "This self-confidence, which was one of Freud's prominent characteristics, was only rarely impaired, and he was doubtless right in tracing it to the security of his mother's love." (Vol. 1, p. 5).

When he was four years old, the family moved to Vienna, where Freud spent the greatest part of his long productive life. He frequently complained about the narrowmindedness and provincialism of the city, but never seriously considered moving. It was only after the Nazis invaded Austria in 1938 that Freud, by now 82 years old and ailing, could be persuaded by friends to leave. He found a hospitable atmosphere in London, but within a short time succumbed to cancer, an illness which he had stoically endured for many years. At the time of his death, in 1939, he had achieved world renown, but recognition had come late in his career and by that time it probably meant little to him.

Describing his formative years, Freud gives this account:

> At the *Gymnasium* (Grammar School) I was at the top of my class for seven years; I enjoyed special privileges there, and had scarcely ever to be examined in class. Although we lived in very limited circumstances, my father insisted that, in my choice of a profession, I should follow my own inclinations alone. Neither at that time, nor indeed in my later life, did I feel any particular predilection for the career of a doctor. I was moved, rather, by a sort of curiosity, which was, however, directed more toward human concerns than toward natural objects; nor had I grasped the importance of observation as one of the best means of gratifying it. . . . At the same time, the theories of Darwin, which were then of topical interest, strongly attracted me, for they held out hopes of an extraordinary advance in our understanding of the world; and it was hearing Goethe's beautiful essay on Nature read aloud at a popular lecture . . . just before I left school that decided me to become a medical student.
>
> When, in 1873, I first joined the University, I experienced some appreciable disappointments. Above all, I

found that I was expected to feel myself inferior and an alien because I was a Jew. I refused absolutely to do the first of these things. I have never been able to see why I should feel ashamed of my descent, or as people were beginning to say, of my 'race.' I put up, without much regret, with my non-acceptance into the community; for it seemed to me that in spite of this exclusion an active fellow-worker could not fail to find some nook or cranny in the framework of humanity. These first impressions at the University, however, had one consequence which was afterwards to prove important; for at an early age I was made familiar with the fate of being in the Opposition. . . . The foundations were thus laid for a certain degree of independence of judgment.
"An Autobiographical Study," pp. 8-9.

Freud recorded that he was "decidedly negligent" in pursuing his medical studies, but eventually he was awarded the degree of Doctor of Medicine (in 1881). During his stay at the Medical School his interest had turned to physiological research and he had apprenticed himself to Ernst Brücke, an outstanding physiologist, for whom he had the highest admiration and respect. Having shown promise as a researcher, Freud would have preferred to embark on a career in scientific research, but financial considerations led him to enter medical practice. In this way he began to study nervous diseases (then the term for mental disorders). Since in Vienna there were few specialists and few opportunities to learn, Freud conceived the plan of obtaining a University appointment as Lecturer on Nervous Diseases and applying for a fellowship to study abroad. This plan was successful and Freud received a grant of $250 to study under the great Jean-Martin Charcot in Paris. Charcot was one of the foremost authorities on diseases of the nervous system, and had also shown great interest in the study of *hysteria,** a disorder which soon became the starting point for Freud's revolutionary insights.

Miss Anna O. and Early Discoveries

Already in the early 1880's, while working in Brücke's laboratory, Freud had made the acquaintance of a respected physician,

*See the Glossary for definitions of technical terms.

Josef Breuer (1842-1925) who, during 1880-1882, had been attending a young woman, who was suffering from hysteria. She had fallen ill during a period of stress, when she was nursing her sick father. The disturbance manifested itself through numerous symptoms, including anesthesia of her right arm and leg, restrictions of her field of vision, difficulty in recognizing people, inability to talk in German (her native tongue), instead of which she only spoke in English, etc. Her condition had grown progressively worse.

While nineteenth century science was much preoccupied with physical causes for any illness, it was apparent that no such causes were at work in the strange symptoms of this patient. On the other hand, hysterical phenomena had been observed for many centuries —indeed as far back as in ancient Greece, when it was thought that the illness was peculiar to women and had something to do with a wanderung uterus. (The term *hystera* means womb.) Little progress had been made, but beginning with Anton Mesmer (1734-1815) greater scientific interest had been shown in hysteria. Mesmer was something of a charlatan and opportunist, but his effort was carried forward by more serious workers, two French physicians, Liébeault (1823-1904) and Bernheim (1840-1919). Gradually, there emerged an awareness that patients suffering from hysteria were extremely suggestible and that this suggestibility somehow played a part in hysteria as well as in the phenomena of hypnosis. Charcot, on the other hand, although he eventually changed his mind, was convinced for a long time that hysteria must be due to some physical disease process in the nervous system.

What was innovative in Breuer's treatment of this young woman, who under the pseudonym "Miss Anna O." achieved fame in the annals of psychoanalysis? Breuer made the observation that when he hypnotized his patient she was able to recall experiences and events of which she was unaware during her waking state. Furthermore, the feelings she experienced in connection with these events were as vivid as they were painful. When Breuer succeeded in evoking these feelings which seemed to go back to painful memories, inducing his patient to express them, he found that upon awakening from her hypnotic state, she was greatly relieved. Repeated application of this technique resulted in marked improvement, which turned out to be lasting. The "talking cure," as Anna O. called it, had been born.

While there is a great distance between this case history and modern psychoanalysis, several important insights were gained:

(1) There evidently was a relationship between hysterical symptoms and hypnosis;

(2) Feelings of which the patient was unaware and which she could not express in the waking state could be brought to awareness during hypnosis, that is, they were previously unconscious but continued to exert an influence on the patient's mental life;

(3) There was some relationship between painful feelings and hysterical symptoms, and the expression of these feelings led to a diminution of the symptoms;

(4) There must be some force within the patient that pushes these feelings out of awareness (subsequently called *repression*);

(5) There must be some barrier in the patient's mind that keeps these feelings from becoming conscious (that is, there exists a *defense* against painful feelings, which shows itself as a seemingly paradoxical *resistance* to cure);

(6) These forces are pitted against each other, giving rise to an *intrapsychic conflict;*

(7) Painful feelings, if denied proper expression, can be converted into physical symptoms (hence the term *conversion* reaction), and this process is reversible, as was true under hypnotic treatment; and

(8) The patient's relationship to the doctor was important in effecting a cure.

This last factor was not given much prominence in Breuer's first account—beyond the implied statement that the patient trusted her physician—but later on Breuer admitted to Freud the disturbing observation that toward the end of the treatment she expressed erotically tinged feelings toward her doctor and perhaps even made some overt sexual advances toward him. To anticipate, Breuer apparently was shocked by these reactions (later on called *transference*) which occurred with some regularity in other patients as well, and it is likely that this factor, more than any other, subsequently deterred him from further research in the field.

Breuer related this remarkable treatment to Freud in November, 1882, who was greatly impressed by it. This despite the fact that his principal interests at the time centered around the anatomy of the nervous system. Later, when studying under Charcot, he mentioned the episode to him, but the Frenchman showed little interest.

Returning to Vienna in 1886, Freud began to specialize in nervous diseases, and many of the patients who consulted him were suffering from disturbances similar to those of Anna O. Freud was discouraged since little could be done for these patients, beyond rest, massage, immersion in water, and the application of mild electric currents. Thus, remembering Breuer's early success, he returned to hypnosis: "During the last few weeks," he wrote to a friend in 1887, "I have taken up hypnosis and have had all sorts of small but remarkable successes."

The work continued, and in 1893 Breuer and Freud published a joint paper, which was followed by a fuller account, *Studies on Hysteria,** in 1895. This volume was of epochal significance because, in addition to numerous case histories, it presented the first full statement of a theory of neurosis.

This theory basically was simple: An experience which is accompanied by a strong emotion (affect) is usually overcome when the emotion is adequately expressed. A hysterical symptom, on the other hand, is formed when (for reasons which were not clearly spelled out at the time) the affect becomes "strangulated." Barred from direct expression, the affect charge finds a devious route, giving rise to a hysterical symptom. When under hypnosis the process is reversed, and the feeling is recalled and expressed, the symptom disappears. The process by which this feat is accomplished was called *abreaction,* and the cure was called *catharsis,* a draining off of emotional energies.

As time went on, Freud became impressed with the importance of sexuality as a factor in hysteria and other neuroses. Originally he thought that sexual urges became "dammed up" in hysteria, and that this process results in anxiety, which seemed to be always present. As his theories developed, he placed increasing weight on the sexual drive (the word "drive" comes closer to the German word *Trieb* than the term *"instinct"* which became common in English translations) as a cause in neurotic disturbances. This emphasis on sex alienated the Viennese scientific community, including Breuer, who withdrew more and more from collaboration. Freud likewise was ostracized by other colleagues. Significantly, it was during this period of almost complete isolation (roughly from 1890 to 1905) that Freud made his most important discoveries. It was a period of incredible productivity. Devoting 10-12 hours a day to seeing patients, Freud did most of his writing

*References to Freud's works will be found in Suggestions for Further Reading.

at night, and in addition carried on an extensive correspondence. The courage and determination that characterized his life and work during this period bespeak a man of great stature. Freud's personal life during this period was rather undramatic. Shortly after returning from France, and following a long engagement, he had married a Jewish girl from Hamburg, Martha Bernays. Jones reports: "Frau Professor, as she became a few years later, never became a real Viennese. She retained her rather precise Hamburg speech, and never adopted the easygoing Viennese ways. She had been as much German as Jewish and that had certain advantages in broadening the family atmosphere. Freud had weaned her from the Jewish orthodoxy in which she had been brought up, and religion played no part in the household. But when she was very old, after her husband's death, she would find interest in discussing Jewish customs and festivals with anyone of a similar cast of thought." (Vol. I, p. 152)

The Freuds had six children, and by all accounts Freud was a devoted father and husband. Early in his marriage he wrote in a letter: "We live pretty happily in steadily increasing unassumingness. When we hear the baby laugh we imagine it is the loveliest thing that can happen to us. I am not ambitious and do not work very hard (sic)." In 1891 the family moved to the well-known address of 19 Berggasse, which remained home for forty-seven years. One of the children, Anna, followed in her father's footsteps and gained world-wide recognition for her psychological work with children.

Psychoanalysis is Born

The book *Studies on Hysteria* actually marks the beginning of psychoanalysis, although the term was not used by Freud until a year later (1896). Prior to this time, he spoke of "Breuer's cathartic method," and occasionally of "psychical analysis." By 1896, Freud had made some notable changes in the original technique.

For one thing, he had given up the use of hypnosis. He had found that some patients could not be hypnotized readily, and the results at other times had been disappointing. Secondly, he had observed that, while hypnosis suspended the patient's *resistance* to recalling painful feelings and memories, the gains were only temporary. Thirdly, he had a temperamental distaste for the magical connotations that always surrounded the hypnotic state.

Instead he modified the technique, asking the patients simply to report as faithfully and unreservedly as possible what occurred to them while in his presence. To keep distractions to a minimum and to insure the greatest possible relaxation, he asked the patient to recline on a couch, sitting behind him, out of his field of vision. He had also noted that when the patients diligently followed what came to be known as *"the fundamental rule,"* their associations regularly began to turn to personal and troublesome matters, ultimately leading to the core of their neurotic difficulties. The new *method of free association* (although the associations were not "free" in the usual sense) was as simple as it was ingenious. The term psychoanalysis as a method treatment is inseparable from the technique of free association.

Psychoanalysis, however, has at least two additional meanings, which soon came to the fore. The first, as we have seen, grew out of the treatment of hysteria, and to this date, psychoanalysis is identified as a specific and specialized form of psychotherapy.

The second meaning, while related to the first, is nevertheless a different one. Psychoanalysis, in this sense, is a method for investigating the working of the human mind, and as such constitutes a remarkable breakthrough in psychological research. Here for the first time was a technique for gaining access to layers of the mind which had hitherto been hidden from direct observation, and which provided highly revealing insights into the origins of the human personality as well as the causes of neurotic conflicts. Thus psychoanalysis in the hands of Freud gradually led to a new understanding and appreciation of the tremendous importance of early childhood in shaping the human personality. The role of sexual impulses was accorded particular emphasis, and Freud's *Three Essays on The Theory of Sexuality,* first published in 1905, represented a signal contribution. It also earned him the undeserved reputation of a pan-sexualist. The hostility and vituperation that descended upon his head from philosophy, religion, psychiatry, and other quarters were characterized by an intensity that is hard to put into words. It is one of the ugly chapters in science around the turn of the century, but a fate not uncommonly meted out to innovators in the history of science. Germany, foreshadowing a later era of intolerance, was in the forefront of these attacks. As Freud observed: "Psychoanalysis brings out the worst in everyone."

The third meaning, again related to the two preceding ones,

refers to psychoanalysis as a theory of personality. Freud, as has been noted, started as a laboratory scientist, who initially showed little interest in psychology. However, searching for a method to treat hysterical patients he was brought face-to-face with the mainsprings of the human mind. By the end of the century he still had not given up hope of reducing psychological phenomena to the laws of physics and chemistry, but eventually he made a clean break and became a psychological investigator who attempted to explain psychological phenomena in psychological terms. Again, this was an achievement of the first order, which is not always fully appreciated.

A New View of the Mind

The road which his observations forced him to travel led from seemingly mysterious symptoms for which no one had any sensible explanations to an inquiry into their origins, which in turn pointed the way to early childhood and the formation of the human personality. Thus psychoanalysis had ceased to be a method of treatment for hysteria and had become a theory of the human personality.

In this journey Freud observed the remarkable resemblance and continuity between abnormal and so-called normal states. His attention was drawn to the study of dreams, slips of the tongue, jokes, and similar commonplace phenomena, to which previously few people had given serious thought. His *magnum opus, The Interpretation of Dreams,* demonstrated the intimate relationship between the formation of dreams and neurotic symptoms. Published in 1900, it first attracted little attention. In analyzing the forces at work in dreams Freud drew heavily on his own, giving many examples.* Within a few years, this work was followed by *The Psychopathology of Everyday Life* (1901) and *Jokes and their Relation to the Unconscious* (1905). Together with the *Three Essays,* these works firmly established a truly revolutionary view of

---

*In a postscript to his autobiography, written in 1935, we find these rather caustic remarks: "The public has no claim to learn any more of my personal affairs—of my struggles, my disappointments, and my successes. I have in any case been more open and frank in some of my writings (such as *The Interpretation of Dreams* and *The Psychopathology of Everyday Life*) than people usually are who describe their lives for their contemporaries or for posterity. I have had small thanks for it, and from my experience I cannot recommend anyone to follow my example" (p. 73).

mental life, underscoring its lawfulness, meaningfulness, and intricacy.

Freud continued to write at a prolific pace, but he rarely matched the brilliant insights of this early period. Rather, many of his later publications are elaborations, reformulations, and applications of psychoanalytic thought to art, literature, religion, and other fields. Never having held a very optimistic view of mankind, Freud became increasingly disillusioned toward the end of his life; however, he never lost faith in the ultimate victory of rationality. It is also significant that at the end of his life he returned to the problems of therapy, which had first engaged his attention.

While working in almost complete isolation for a number of years, Freud gradually attracted a growing circle of collaborators and followers. The names of Alfred Adler, a Viennese physician, and Carl Gustav Jung, a Swiss psychiatrist, each of whom subsequently developed theories of his own, deserve particular mention. Lifelong friendships with Ernest Jones, a British psychiatrist, and Sándor Ferenczi, a Hungarian, demonstrated Freud's ability to inspire allegiance and loyalty.

Informal meetings among the young group of psychoanalysts were first held at Freud's home, but beginning in 1908 international psychoanalytic congresses were held regularly, the first one being in Salzburg, Austria. Psychoanalytic societies were founded in numerous countries, journals devoted to the budding science were published, and Freud's fame gradually spread. In 1909, in response to an invitation from the eminent American psychologist G. Stanley Hall, Freud made his only visit to the United States, lecturing at Clark University. He was deeply gratified by the cordial reception accorded him, and while he never developed a deep affection for America, he found the atmosphere on this side of the Atlantic immeasurably more objective and tolerant than in his native Austria.

His style of writing, both lucid and simple, undoubtedly played an important part in spreading his ideas. It is somewhat ironic that while his scientific contributions received no official recognition during his lifetime, he was awarded the Goethe Prize for literature by the city of Frankfurt am Main in 1930.

First, and foremost, Freud was a scientist. He religiously followed the advice of his master, Charcot: to look at the same things again and again until they begin to speak. He was reared in the scientific tradition, and his theories never lost touch with the observations upon which they were ultimately based. Nor did he delude himself that he had discovered ultimate truths; indeed, he was keenly aware of the tentativeness and tenuousness which characterize all scientific theories. On the other hand, he took justifiable pride in having advanced the frontiers of human knowledge to an unprecedented degree. He regarded psychoanalysis as a scientific discovery, but also largely as his own creation.

From a science which initially was chiefly concerned with unconscious processes, psychoanalysis had become a way of understanding the total human personality — in its normal as well as abnormal manifestations. But in addition to being a science, psychoanalysis also had become a view of man, a *Weltanschauung*. While extolling the power of reason and rationality, Freud had at the same time shown their limitations. He had dealt a severe blow to man's egocentrism, much as Galileo had shattered the view of the earth as the center of the universe. Mankind, as Freud observed, never forgave him for having disturbed its sleep.

Above all, he was a sworn enemy of deception and dissimulation in all its forms — both conscious and unconscious. This uncompromising fervor to explore the recesses of the human mind, to forge ahead with uncanny determination and singlemindedness of purpose, yet tempering his insights with compassion for man's fallibility — these are perhaps the most outstanding qualities of Freud's genius.

CHAPTER 2

The Mental
Apparatus

Psychoanalysis as a Psychological Theory

Psychoanalytic theory is a *psychological* theory, that is, its concern is with the understanding of psychological phenomena in psychological terms. It does not attempt to reduce them to the laws of another science like physiology but treats them as irreducible. For example, a person who is anxious may have an accelerated heart rate; he may have palmar sweating; and his breathing my be irregular. It is possible to note these physiological changes and even to measure them quite accurately. However, they do not *explain* the person's mental state nor do they teach us much about the control of anxiety, which remains a psychological phenomenon. It is often thought that explanations of psychological phenomena in physiological terms are "more basic," and Freud himself, at one point in his career, attempted seriously to cast his theory in terms of neuroanatomy and neurophysiology, but he abandoned this attempt, restricting himself to efforts at understanding psychological phenomena in psychological terms. For this reason, too, Freud was emphatic in his belief that psychoanalytic theory belongs to the field of psychology, not to medicine or psychiatry, which themselves are applications of basic biological sciences like anatomy, physiology, biochemistry, and the like. To be sure, psychoanalysis recognizes that any form of human behavior has its physical, physiological, social (and other) aspects, but its focus rests on the psychological representations.

Instinct and Wish

The concept of *drive,* which is basic to psychoanalytic theory, illustrates this point. Freud (1915) defined an instinctual drive (*Trieb*) ". . . as a concept on the frontier between the mental and the somatic, as the physical representative of stimuli originating from within the organism and reaching the mind, as a measure of the demand made upon the mind for work in consequence of its connection with the body." The energies which are operative within the human organism are ultimately physical energies, but psycho-analysis as a psychological science is concerned with the manner in which they are represented psychologically. A *wish,* therefore, is a psychological concept which mirrors a physiological state which impels the organism to action. The concept *instinct* is utterly removed from direct inspection; however, a wish may appear in awareness as an impelling force. A wish thus is the psychological counterpart of an underlying instinct, but it may be only a feeble and inadequate representation of the instinct. Instinctual energy (called *libido)* is the hypothetical driving force which is conceptualized as motivating all human behavior.

It is important to point out that the psychoanalytic concept "wish" is not coextensive with the commonsense term. For one thing, many wishes, seen in the psychoanalytic framework, never reach consciousness and are often not clearly formulated in terms of a subject, predicate, and object. Secondly, they are often not pleasurable in the ordinary sense. Rather they have a primitive, driving, and primordial quality. Frequently, they are crude, and uncivilized. Characteristically, they have sexual and/or aggressive connotations. Many of them are quite unacceptable to the conscious part of the personality.

The Id

Wishes, as psychic representatives of instinctual drives, originate in the most primitive layer of the mental apparatus, which is conceptualized as the *Id.* The id is closest to the instinctual drives and may be viewed as an inexhaustable reservoir of wishes, impulses, and strivings which continuously press for discharge through some form of action of the organism. This discharge results in tension release which is spoken of as "pleasure." The id may be crudely viewed as a kettle which is continually kept under pressure by the biological drives of the organism. Strivings originating in the id are partially inborn, partially the result of the biological maturation of the organism. They have no regard for reality, the rights of other persons, or, for that matter, the welfare of the person owning them. They are blind, often mutually contradictory, and devoid of rationality. For example, a wish to kill a beloved person may live side by side in the id with the wish to possess that person sexually; a desire to be cuddled and fondled like a baby may coexist with a ruthless drive for self-assertion. As Freud put it, the id is "a cauldron of seething emotions" which is active throughout the person's lifetime, and difficult to influence or modify.

Freud regarded the newborn infant as largely dominated by the id. Everyday observation certainly confirms that the infant's needs are imperious and they tolerate very little delay. When the infant is hungry, he must be fed almost instantly. Everyone is familiar with the massive bodily reaction of a small infant when he is hungry, soiled, or otherwise uncomfortable. He gets red in the face, tenses up, and violently reacts to the slightest frustration of his inborn needs. He has no regard for the fact that the mother may be busy with an older sibling or pursuing other duties. He operates according to the formula: I-want-what-I-want-when-I-want-it-and-I-will-not-take-no-for-an-answer. In addition to his biological needs, the small infant needs warmth, comfort, and the closeness of another person. In short, he needs to be mothered. Research by René Spitz and others has shown that infants who do not get this mothering literally do not survive. The enormity of the infant's demands are largely rooted in his biological immaturity which determines his dependency on adults. Indeed, the human infant's prolonged dependency on his family is a significant source of neurotic problems to which man is prone. To have demonstrated this fact is one of Freud's lasting achievements.

We must reiterate that the infant's needs are exceedingly strong; they must be gratified with a minimum of delay; and frustration of any sort gives rise to massive bodily reactions of uncontrollable anger and rage. Gratification leads to pleasurable feelings (tension release), whereas frustration leads to the building up of tension, which the infant experiences (it must be inferred) as painful and unpleasurable. These two primitive forms of experience are deeply ingrained in the person's id and form the basis of his later development: an infant whose needs have been largely met with kindness, tolerance, and understanding will, other things being equal, grow up into a more contented and happy adult than an infant whose needs—both biological and psychological—have been chronically frustrated almost from the beginning. Fortunately, most people have had the good fortune of being brought up by mothers who, at least in the early months of the child's existence, have been capable of meeting his needs to a very appreciable extent. The child thus learns to experience a sense of basic trust, which is the most precious asset in meeting adversity in later life. Finally, it is to be noted that the id is closest to the biological needs of the human organism with which indeed it is inextricably intertwined; it is concerned with the organism's survival; and, as such, it represents the core of the person which is completely self-centered and concerned with his own gratification. Most of the id's contents are completely and forever *unconscious*, but the unconscious, in Freudian theory, is not synonymous or coterminous with the id.

The Ego

The ego, the second "agency" of the mental apparatus, serves primarily the organism's adaptive function; that is, it mediates between its biological and psychological needs on the one hand and external reality on the other.

In Freud's original conception, the ego was regarded as taking its origin from the id, from which it was seen as gradually evolving and whose energies it was thought to "borrow." From this conception derived the metaphor of the rider (ego) who is controlling and directing the movement of his horse (id), on whose energies he is dependent. During the last twenty-five years, notably since Freud's death, this conception has been seriously questioned. Now it is assumed that rudiments of the ego are evident even in the very small infant, and that certain functions of the organism (e.g., perception) lie, from the very beginning, outside the domain of the id, that is, they are not drive-dominated. While these newer views have important theoretical implications, it suffices to note that even the very small child is not *completely* dominated by the instinctual impulses of the id, and that he exercises certain rudimentary psychological functions which, as far as can be determined, do not serve the immediate gratification of an instinctual drive. Playful and exploratory behavior which is seen in very small children is a good illustration of this point.

The ego gradually develops under the influence of the child's early experience with significant adults, particularly his mother (or mother substitute). Probably one of the first distinctions the child learns is a dim recognition between himself and the external world. He learns to differentiate between "inside" and "outside," between things that are part of his body and things that are separate from it. Part of this lesson is learned through frustration. For example, he finds that the movements of his mother are by no means completely under his control. Whereas crying usually brings the mother to his side, this is not always the case, and the mother is experienced as having concerns other than the child's needs. Even at a very early age he begins to tolerate a certain amount of delay. He can and does learn to wait for the bottle or the maternal breast at least a short while without flying into a fit of uncontrolled rage, and he learns that even though delay is inevitable, the gratification quite regularly is provided. As a result, he builds up within himself certain psychic structures which enable him to tolerate delay of gratification. This, to an important degree, is precisely the ego's function: to take into account the *reality* of a situation; to be able to *anticipate;* to tolerate *delays;* to put up with frustration; to adapt to the demands and needs of others; and to modify the needs of the organism in such a way that control become possible. This means that from the beginning the budding ego begins to exert a controlling and curbing influence over the pressing needs that emanate from the id.

The ego, then, is the reasonable, rational aspect of the human personality which adapts to the external world and seeks to assure the survival of the person in a world populated by other people who have their own rights, needs, and motives. The ego, too, attempts to bring about gratification of the organism's needs, but within the framework of accepted standards and external demands.

The ego is conceived of as the executive apparatus of the human personality which listens both to its inner promptings as well as to the outer world. It maintains control over motor movements; it initiates motor action or inhibits it. It benefits from experience and draws on life experience to anticipate the consequences of particular acts. It stores life experience in memory traces, and through its knowledge of the external world continually attempts to steer a course which it considers to be in keeping with the welfare of the organism in its transactions with the external world.

The ego, in sum, represents the distillate of the person's life experience which has become internalized. It is viewed as a mental structure (organization) which makes possible independence, autonomy, and self-direction. Depending on the character of the person's life experience, particularly during the earliest years of life, the ego is a reasonable replica of reality as it was mediated by the parents who serve as the first models. To the extent that the parents are deficient or distorted mediators of what reality is like, the child's ego correspondingly becomes warped and distorted. Ideally, there is a close match between the parents' egos, external reality as represented by the culture within which the family lives, and the child's evolving ego. In actuality, the parents are never perfect models, but, as may be readily seen, unless their standards are a reasonable facsimile of what the child may later expect from others, they have prepared him very poorly for life. For example, a child who has been excessively pampered by a parent invariably will encounter grave difficulties when he makes the discovery that teachers, schoolmates, and other people are not inclined to behave in accordance with his unrealistic expectations. Contrariwise, a child whose parents have been unduly critical and perfectionistic in their expectations, may find that others are much more tolerant and accepting. The reason that the ego does not always readily profit from later life experience is partially to be found in the third intrapsychic agency, the superego, which we shall next consider. However, it should be pointed out that while the ego, according to psychoanalytic theory, includes all of the conscious self, there are segments of the ego which are not accessible to consciousness. For example, the processes by which the ego defends itself against threatening impulses from the id, are largely unconscious: The ability to observe one's feelings and actions and to reflect upon them is obviously a uniquely human quality. No other organism is capable of saying "I."

The Superego

The third major "agency" of the psychic apparatus is the superego which, in terms of the child's emotional development, is acquired last. The superego coincides to some extent with the commonsense conception of "conscience," but it remained for Freud to work out its dynamics and to demonstrate its pervasive influence over the person's emotional life.

The superego essentially represents the precipitate of the parents' values, ideals, prohibitions, injunctions, standards, and the like. The child acquires and internalizes these at a rather early age and makes them his own. In technical language, he *introjects* them. How does this come about? In general terms the process is mediated by the child's dependence on his parents for approval and love. He feels "good" if he senses that he enjoys his parents' approval; and he feels "bad" (guilty, ashamed), if they disapprove. The parents, as can be seen, control the system of rewards and punishments by which the child orients himself in the world. This system eventually serves him to exercise independent control over his impulses, wishes, and strivings. The parents' standards, of course, largely represent the standards of the culture (although there are great individual variations), and the internalization of these standards ultimately makes possible civilized living in a society· To be sure, internal superego controls are not perfect, as demonstrated by the fact that society employs policemen to enforce its prohibitions; on the other hand, a person's superego is often far more severe and harsh than is required by the institutions of society.

From the above presentation it might be concluded that the superego is a rational and reasonable part of the human personality which enforces law and order within the individual as well as in his relations with the outside world. Unfortunately, nothing could be farther from the truth. In part, the superego certainly *is* a reasonable arbiter concerned with the task of maintaining amicable relations between the welfare of the individuals, his impulses, and the demands of the external world. Often, however, it is a tyrant, a despot, whose operations are characterized by a good deal of sadism and cruelty. The reasons for this state of affairs are complex, but a good deal of light has been shed on the problem through clinical observation, particularly through the treatment of neurotic patients. Basically, the reasons have to do with (1) the intensity of small child's needs, wishes, and demands, (2) the true character of the parents' attitudes and reactions to infantile behavior, and (3) distortions which the child introduces by misinterpreting the parents' attitudes on the basis of his limited understanding of social reality.

For example, it is true that parents are often exceedingly intolerant of behavior in their children which strikes them as "infantile" or "immature." Any parent knows that certain actions of his child may infuriate him no end, and that the parental re-action is totally out of keeping with the severity of the misbehavior. Investigation not uncommonly reveals that such performances remind the parent of tendencies in himself which he needs to control and suppress. In these circumstances, punishment that is meted out may be particularly cruel and harsh, because the parent's own superego demands strong retributive action. In this way, too, the child comes to assume identical attitudes toward himself and the tendencies of which the parent so vehemently disapproves. In short, he *identifies* with his parents—a process about which psychoanalysis has a great deal to say, but which is still not very well understood.

However, it is frequently found that children whose parents were rather mild have extraordinarily harsh and punitive superegos. The explanation, at least in part, lies in the distortions which the child himself introduces and which may have little to do with the reality of the situation. His own fantasies and wishes often supply the material from which the superego is built. For instance, a little boy may fear that the punishment for masturbation is castration, irrespective of whether the parents have made or implied such a threat. Rather the child's fear is based on his own primitive fantasies which are traceable to his inborn destructive impulses. These impulses are often seen to have a vicious, sadistic quality. We see, then, that the superego often "collaborates" with the id, and indeed at times makes common cause with it.

At its best, the superego is a helpful guide to the person in his dealings with the outside world, in helping him decide what is "right" and "wrong," in dispensing a feeling of goodness and worthwhileness when the person lives in accordance with the dictates of his superego, and in making him feel guilty if he does not. At its worst, the superego is a cruel, sadistic, unreasonable tyrant, which metes out punishment for minor transgressions and treats them as major crimes, and which, in the extreme, makes it impossible for the person to derive any kind of enjoyment from life.

The superego, despite its primitive components, is modifiable on the basis of the individual's life experience. Teachers, admired persons, and the like, to some extent supersede the early parental influence and mold the person's ideals, standards, and values. Everyone carries within himself an *ego ideal*, a mental picture of the kind of person he would like to be, although, like any ideal, it remains an unrealizable goal. This ego ideal is importantly determined by superego forces·

In summary the mental apparatus, in psychoanalytic psychology, is conceptualized as consisting of three "agencies," the id, the ego, and the superego. The three forces, while having distinctive implications for the functioning of the total personality, are always interacting, never separate. They are frequently in conflict with each other, and these conflicts are seen in chronic and exaggerated form in the psychoneuroses.

CHAPTER **3**

The Stages of Personality Development

Initially, Freud was primarily interested in providing a psychological explanation of neurotic symptoms and in devising a technique for treating them. Indeed, the second objective first attracted his attention to the problem of neurotic disturbances, although he soon became interested in developing psychological theories that might have wider applicability. His genius enabled him to realize that neuroses were not "diseases of the nervous system," as nineteenth century psychiatry tended to view them, but as deviations cr complications traceable to the total pattern of the person's emotional development. It was one of Freud's great achievements to discern *continuity* and *orderly development* in each individual's emotional maturation. Thus, emotional disturbances in adult life were no longer seen as quirks or disease entities for which no rational explanation could be found; rather Freud demonstrated that they could be understood as *logical outcomes of a disturbed childhood*. Hence he arrived at the dictum: no adult neurosis without an infantile neurosis. Neurotic symptoms which were so puzzling to the early psychiatrists thus became understandable within the context of the child's early development. Freud's formulations focused heavily on the child's early love relationships and the stages which he delineated (oral, anal, phallic, and genital) were seen as waystations in the evolution of the sexual instinct. In more recent years, chiefly under the influence of Erik Erikson,* the drive development has been placed more squarely within the totality of the child's maturation, environmental influences, and cultural milieu. These, assuredly, were never disregarded by Freud, although his emphasis rested on the development of the drives, which, at least by some people, were seen as unfolding almost without regard for socio-environmental factors. Freud's formulations to some extent invited this erroneous conception.

The development of the child's drives certainly does not occur in a vacuum. As the child matures, he has to meet certain challenges and crises which force him to come to terms both with the motive forces within and the expectations of his parents (and indirectly society) without. These challenges that are posed by the requirements for socialization create problems that many children fail to resolve in adequate ways. Freud saw the principal problem in the early budding of the child's *sexual impulses,* and the conflicts arising therefrom. Later he came to see that the separation of the child's close relationship to his mother, the demands for weaning and, subsquently, the imposed *control* by the outside world over the child's bowel functions represent developmental problems of equal, if not greater importance.

In some sense, the difference between Freud's conception and Erikson's is one of emphasis. One can (with Freud) think of drive energies which undergo maturation and development, and which invest various "zones": first, the mouth; second, the anal sphincter; and third, the genitals. Stimulation of these zones is regarded as giving rise to pleasurable (erotogenic) sensations. Or, one can (with Erikson) think of the human organism as passing through several stages of development. Each of these stages has its focal point, which may become so pleasurable that the individual is unwilling to give it up. In technical terms, he may remain *fixated* at a given level. The mouth thus is the earliest pleasure zone, and to some extent early oral pleasures (sucking) are retained in modified forms throughout life (e.g., smoking, kissing, etc.).

Certainly, the small infant's pleasurable sensations undoubtedly derive to a large measure from stimulation of the mouth and the intake of nourishment· So, one can speak of this stage as the

*Erik H. Erikson. *Childhood and Society.* New York: W. W. Norton, 1950.

"oral period". But this period is also characterized by immaturity, the need to be taken care of by others, the wish to be passive, to "take in" all that is pleasurable and to "spit out" all that tastes bad. The focal point of the child's personality organization at this period is not necessarily the mouth per se but *the total constellation of immaturity, dependency, the wish to be mothered, the pleasure of being held, the enjoyment of human closeness and warmth.* All of these are characteristic of this period of life. To be sure, Freud was keenly aware of the total picture, but he saw it in terms of unfolding instincts (part of the libido theory) rather than as a broader developmental stage.

The foregoing questions about the value of the libido theory do not detract from Freud's perspicacious conceptions of infantile development and the budding of infantile sexuality around ages three to five. Let us briefly trace this sequence, without neglecting the psycho-social factors that prominently play a part in each.

The Oral Period

As we have already seen, the oral phase characterizes the earliest and in many respects the most critical period of the child's development, for in this period are determined some of the most crucial aspects of the child's personality. Here the foundation is laid for all subsequent developments, and at no time in later life is it possible to influence a person as profoundly and lastingly as during the earliest months of his existence.

The reasons for this enormous malleability lie in the general immaturity of the organism, its utter dependency upon the care, devotion, and love of his parents, without which, in a very literal sense, he could not survive. Every child of course is born with hereditary characteristics that predispose him in a variety of ways. It is also undeniable that hereditary factors play a part in temperamental differences that can be observed even in very small children. Some, as observations show in the nursery, are more active; some are more placid; some seem to be easier to satisfy than others; and some never seem to be satisfied no matter how much loving care and attention is expended upon them. But, as Freud, and many investigators following him, have observed, the mother's attitudes towards the child and his well-being as well as his response—almost from the first day of life—set up a pattern of interaction which is of basic significance in later life.

The importance of the child's experiences during the oral period can hardly be overestimated, and, as more recent clinical studies have shown, this period far overshadows later stages, particularly the Oedipal period, which has gained much wider currency in the public's mind. It seems desirable, therefore, to dwell at somewhat greater length upon this phase of the child's development in order to highlight its pervasive influence upon later personality development and character formation.

From the adult's point of view it is difficult to gain a full appreciation of the intensity of the small child's biological as well as psychological needs, as well as the manner in which these needs are met (or unmet) by the mother or mother substitute. Considerable evidence has been amassed by direct observations of infants and their families since the time of Freud, corroborating his theories. Freud himself never studied infants or small children at close range, relying almost exclusively on reconstructions from his clinical work with adult patients.

As has been stated, the child's needs are intense; the slightest frustration may lead to all-encompassing rage; the child is completely self-centered and has no regard for the external world; and his needs must be satisfied promptly if he is to survive. The child, according to Freud, is almost completely under the sway of the id; whether rudiments of the ego are present at birth or not, the ego, as a controlling agency, is exceedingly weak and, for practical purposes, not functional. The most painful experience (trauma), which every human being must undergo, is the act of birth—the separation from the all-protecting environment of the womb. Henceforth, deprivation and frustration become inevitable, and they increase as the child grows older. In the early days of his existence, the child may be fed "on demand," but soon the intervals between feeding periods are stretched, often for the convenience of the parents. The child will at times feel wet, uncomfortable, and in pain. These experiences, too, are part of the "human condition," that is, they are unavoidable.

From the very beginning of life, the infant begins to associate human warmth, the act of being fed, the experience of being held securely in his mother's arms with signs of love, security, and safety in a dangerous and hostile world. To be sure, he cannot verbalize or report his experiences. These formulations are inferences, but there is no doubt that something of this sort must be the basis (substrate) of the child's early life experience. Depending on the manner in which the child's needs are met, he undoubtedly comes to experience the world as a predominantly friendly place (in which love, security, and gratification preponderate over pain, deprivation, and loneliness), or, alternatively, as a frightening cosmos which is characterized by ungivingness, or grudging concessions to the child's needs. The most basic orientations of people toward life, optimism or pessimism, are thus formed at a very early, and never consciously remembered, stage. It may also be seen that the mother's ability to meet her child's needs and consequently to instil in him the experience of being loved plays a crucial part in this development. A child who has been loved will be able to reciprocate and eventually develop into a loving person himself. A child who has gained faith in the reliability and essential lovingness of his mother will become able to trust others, and—more importantly perhaps—himself. Contrariwise, a child on whom the gift of love has been bestowed grudgingly or who, from the very beginning, had to fight for it, will assume a pessimistic and distrustful attitude toward all people. (See the earlier discussion on the formation of basic trust.)

Fortunately, most individuals have received a fair share of maternal love in the earliest days and months of their life, and while frustration becomes the lot of everyone, they have, as it were, a surplus of loving experience. This earliest of experiences forms the cornerstone upon which the human personality is built. It is apparent that an infant who perenially has been "hungry" for food, affection, acceptance, and love, will meet later deprivations with reluctance, and he will forever yearn for an experience of full gratification that was never his. Depressions, for example, when traced to their ultimate origin, are deeply rooted in the small child's feeding experience. But, it is not so much the feeding of nourishment per se but the mother's *attitudes* surrounding the feeding experience which are important.

Of course, the child does not "know" the nature of these experiences, nor can he put them into words, which are not a part of his emotional repertoire. Yet he senses deeply with his whole being the attitudes that are displayed toward him. He *empathizes* with the mother. It must also be noted that the child's self-esteem soon comes to be involved in his early life experience. If he experiences the mother's attitudes and feelings as good, benevolent, gratifying, he comes to see himself as good, worthwhile, and acceptable. In the opposite case, he cannot fail but regard himself as bad, demanding, greedy, and essentially unlovable.

It is a demonstrated fact that these early dispositions are virtually immutable at later stages in the person's life. Clinical experience amply shows that an adult is almost impervious to corrections in these earliest life experiences. Once the die is cast—and it is clear that what is important here is not a single experience but rather a "climate" that persists from day to day, from week to week, from month to month — the individual has acquired an almost unshakable conviction in the "goodness" or "badness" of the world, and a similarly tenacious faith in his own intrinsic goodness or badness. This is the essence of the oral period.

The Anal Period

The oral period, as we have seen, pertains to the earliest phase of the infant's development. No demands are made on him by the external world, and he feels himself to be the center of the universe. Things are given to him without effort on his part, and nothing matters but his own satisfaction. His existence is entirely self-centered.

This picture gradually changes as the child matures biologically, shows increasing recognition and responsiveness to the people around him, and gains increasing control over his skeletal musculature.

As this process continues, the child very slowly becomes socialized. He has learned that there is a difference between himself (as a person or entity) and the external world. He comes to differentiate between other persons and inanimate objects, like tables and chairs, which hurt you if you bump against them, and which don't go away simply by wishing.

Most important are the demands which the parents gradually make with respect to the child's sphincter control. Depending on the child's relationship to his parents, as laid down in the oral period, he is eager and willing to win his parents' approval by complying with their wishes, or he begins stubbornly to resist the imposition of external controls. He also makes the discovery that he can use the musculature of his anal sphincters as a means of social control. That is, he can please his parents by attempting to evacuate his bowels at a time and place appointed by them; or, he can follow his own inclinations in this respect. It is truly remarkable how often bowel training becomes a battleground between parents and children, particularly if the child finds that the parents set great score by his acquiring control over his sphincters, and, if for other reasons, the child feels impelled to engage in warfare with the powerful adults in his environment. Again, the problem seems not so much one of instinctual impulses (as Freud originally postulated) but rather it represents a special and focal aspect of the total child-parent relationship.

Freud correctly recognized, and countless observations have borne him out, that this period (roughly between the first and second years of the child's life) represents his first encounter with the demands and expectations of the outside world. For the first time in his life he is required to relinquish some of his pervasive self-centeredness and egoism (termed *narcissism* in Freud's later writings) and to subordinate his all-encompassing wishes to the demands of reality. His dutiful performance on the toilet earns him the approval and love of his parents, whereas his refusal to perform may lead to their disapprobation and displeasure. If the child has received adequate mothering during the earliest period of his life, he is usually quite willing to put up with the external controls that are gradually being imposed. If, in a deep sense, he has never, rarely, or only sporadically had the experience of real gratification, he will continually yearn for the halcyon days in which rest, passivity, and quiescence seemed the true goals of his existence, and he will fight with all his might against any encroachment upon his "independence" (which is really utter dependence).

Character traits, such as negativism, stubbornness, rigidity, frugality, and parsimony were identified by Freud as belonging to the anal period. In part, these have to do with the value that has been placed by the important figures in the child's world upon giving up the contents of his bowels, but they also reflect the manner in which the child has learned to channel his aggressive, destructive, and sadistic impulses.

The child tends to see his acquiescence to the parental demands and the parting with his bowel contents as a precious gift he is making to his parents. He values highly what was once "his," inside of him, a part of him, and he sees its abandonment as a "loss." Besides, parents often regard the child's feces as "valuable" initially, but soon the child perceives that his inner "treasure" is treated with disgust. Strange as it may seem to the adult mind, the child's successful control over his bowels is a great achievement in socialization, and his "productivity" on the toilet is the prototype of productivity in his later life. This is not to assert, as some critics of Freud's have done, that art and the great achievements of the human spirit are *directly* traceable to the process of elimination. Nothing was further from Freud's mind. However, he did see the *origins* of human productivity, and conversely, the stubborn withholding to which some people are prone, as emanating from this early period of life. A person's attitude toward possessions (including money) and his readiness to share them with or bestow them upon others, are similarly patterned after the interpersonal experiences surrounding the anal period. Finally, the child's sadistic tendencies are woven into the control he begins to exert over his own body and upon the external world. The common observation that angry and destructive impulses are typically expressed in anal terms attests to the deep-seated relation between sadism and the anal function.

The Oedipal Period

Freud differentiated a third phase, called *phallic,* as a precursor to the Oedipus phase. In both sexes, according to Freud, the penis becomes valued as an organ of supreme power, and its possessor, in the child's fantasy, is capable of unlimited achievement, prowess, and success.

Freud's succinct account of the *Oedipus* phase which makes its appearance at age three to four can hardly be improved upon and is therefore quoted:

> With the phallic phase and in the course of it the sexuality of early childhood reaches its height and approaches its decline. Thenceforward boys and girls have different histories. To begin with, both place their intellectual activity at the service of sexual research; both start off from the presumption of the universal presence of the penis. But now the paths of the sexes divide. The boy enters the Oedipus phase; he begins to manipulate his penis and simultaneously has phantasies of carrying out some sort of activity with it in relation to his mother; but at last, owing to the combined effect of à threat of castration and the spectacle of the women's lack of a penis, he experiences the greatest trauma of his life, and this introduces the period of latency with all its attendant consequences. The girl, after vainly attempting

to do the same as the boy, comes to recognize her lack of penis or rather the inferiority of her clitoris, with permanent effects upon the development of her character; and, as a result of this first disappointment in rivalry, she often turns away altogether from sexual life.   (Freud, *Outline*, pp. 29-30).

Freud points out that the various stages do not follow each other in clearcut fashion; rather there is a good deal of overlap, and a phase is never completely superseded. They shade into each other, and in actual life, are always intermingled.

What is important to keep in mind is that the early phases of psychosexual development represent the pattern which the person's sexual life in adulthood will almost inevitably follow. Indeed, it was one of Freud's major contributions to have described in considerable detail and with hitherto unequalled insight the *biphasic* nature of the child's sexual development. The fact that sexual development reaches an early flowering during the child's third or fourth year, but because of his biological and psychological immaturity is destined to endure a protracted period of suppression and delay is at least in part responsible for the difficulties which many people encounter in effecting a smooth transition from childhood to adolescence and adulthood.

The keynote of the Oedipal development is the *delay* of gratification, the ability to tolerate frustration and to transfer erotic feelings from the early objects of one's childhood to nonincestuous ones in later life. The foregoing formula, as can be recognized, also implies a high degree of *renunciation* on the child's part. It is as if fate decreed: True, you (the child) have powerful erotic strivings toward the parent of the opposite sex. These feelings are fueled by the closeness, intimacy, and affection you have received from the parent since the beginning of your life. But, unfortunately, this budding of erotic feelings is doomed. It cannot find gratification in relation to the person toward whom it is directed. You first have to grow up, become mature, and independent before you can find a person who will approximate but, regrettably, never equal the parent of whom you have become so fond and to whom you are so firmly attached. The exercise of sexuality on the part of the immature human individual is ·impossible; it is forbidden; and it must be contained. You have to come to terms with it; suppress it for the time being; find substitute gratifications; and, to some extent, drive underground (*repress*) a significant part of it.

The successful resolution of this conflict guarantees the person a strong foundation for mental health; failure, with monotonous regularity, lays the groundwork for neurotic problems in later life. Again, solutions must not be thought of as occurring on an all-or-none basis. It is always a matter of *degree*. Since residues of an "unresolved Oedipus complex" may be found in all persons, the question turns upon the *extent* to which it exerts an influence over the total personality in the sense of determining relationships with members of the same and the opposite sex in later life.

Freud demonstrated that the successful resolution of the Oedipus period subordinates the person's sexual and erotic strivings to the genital zone, which serves to amalgamate oral, anal, and genital impulses. Again, this is never wholly successful—only approximately so. Similarly, the "genital personality" is an abstract ideal which does not exist in reality. Everyone, to a greater or lesser extent, bears in his emotional development the scars of the conflicts he underwent in his relationships with his father and mother, as well as the identifications he made with the figures of his childhood. More will be said about the role of the Oedipus problem in a later chapter.

Latency, Adolescence, and Adulthood

Psychoanalytic psychology has distinctly less to say about the child's personality development following the Oedipal period. Once the storms of early childhood have been weathered a relatively calmer period sets in. Beginning around age five or six, the so-called latency phase occurs, leading to preadolescence and puberty. During the latency phase the child is still dependent on his family, but by this time he has developed a complex personality organization which permits him to make the transition from the sheltered atmosphere of the home to the demands of school. Many significant experiences of early childhood become overlaid and are often repressed. The child learns to master a wide variety of skills—controlling his body, learning to adapt to and get along with contemporaries, etc. Latency must not be regarded as a period without stress, and it is often difficult for the parents to appreciate fully the many problems the child has to solve. He is faced with competition, the need to achieve, and to find his place in a world of equals, who insist upon their rights and privileges. No longer is the child a central figure in a protective and protecting family, but he must spend increasingly long hours under discipline, and his needs must be subordinated to those of the peer group. He must learn to accept responsibility, he must conform, and yet he must also safeguard his individuality. He identifies with the ideals and values of same-sexed peers, and for some years shows little interest in the opposite sex. He tests the standards of the home against those of the peer group; he will find that the parents are not the infallible figures he had once pictured them to be; and he encounters other adults, some of whom come to serve as better ideals than the parents. Much of this growth process, while almost imperceptible, is none-theless real.

Adolescence intensifies the separation from the parents and places increasing value upon conformity to the peer culture. The relative peace of the latency period often is replaced by rebellion against tradition and parental values. Biological maturation con-fronts the adolescent with the problem of managing his or her sexual urges, which now emerge with particular intensity. Repres-sion, as was true in childhood, no longer is the answer, but reality imposes further delays and restrictions upon sexual expression. However, most adolescents somehow struggle through to a state of relative stability.

When has the individual achieved adulthood? Maturity is always relative, and as one expert observed, most people in our culture always remain adolescents in their emotional development. To quote one authority, the criteria of adulthood include: "Dis-appearance of the turmoil, uncertainty and conflict of adoles-cence, the appearance of emotional control and general predict-ability, the establishment of self-confidence and self-respect, a willingness to accept adult responsibilities even within the frame-work of economic dependence, and a self-assertive independence of thinking and judgment. These are the marks of emotional maturity, of the channeling of sexual and aggressive drives, of adult ego integration, of the stabilization of superego functioning — in providing both self-criticism and self-esteem — and of a realistic construction of a person's external and internal worlds."* It is readily seen that this is an ideal state reached by few persons.

---

*Cameron, Norman, *Personality Development and Psychopathology* (Boston: Houghton Mifflin, 1963), pp. 111-12.

CHAPTER 4

Psychodynamics:
Further Considerations

In preceding chapters we discussed the three major "agencies" of the psychic apparatus—the ego, the id, and the superego. We have also attempted to delineate their respective functions in the individual's adaptation to his internal environment as well as to the outside world. Indeed, the ego as well as the superego are largely a precipitate of the growing individual's transactions with the outside world. In other words, the person profits from experience—he learns—and the products of this learning are incorporated, stored, or made a part of his mental equipment.

Furthermore, a distinction has been made between consciousness and the dynamic unconscious. Portions of the ego are conscious although the ego and consciousness are by no means coextensive. The id is almost completely unconscious. Large segments of the superego, too, are unconscious. For most people, the concept of the dynamic unconscious is difficult to grasp, part of the reason being that such understanding demands the acceptance of the notion that all of us are continually governed by forces within ourselves of which we are completely unaware and over which we have no conscious control. Historically, this major discovery of Freud's was a bitter pill to swallow for nineteenth century man, who had prided himself in the supremacy of reason and the intellect. As Freud pointed out, it was his fate to strike a blow against man's inflated notions of his rational powers, which was analogous to the changing conceptions of the earth as the center of the universe in the days of Galileo and Kepler.

Conscious, Preconscious, and Unconscious

Freud, too, made an important distinction between *conscious, preconscious,* and *unconscious* (the lay term "subconscious" has no specific meaning in Freudian psychology, although it probably refers most frequently to unconscious phenomena). The concept of consciousness requires little elaboration because it substantially coincides with the commonsense definition of the term. Preconscious describes a mental quality which again is familiar to everyday experience. Anyone's life experience includes a host of memories, associations, etc. which are typically outside of awareness but which can potentially enter the field of consciousness on a moment's notice. Asked about landmarks in the city of their birth, most people can actively recall a large number. These memories and past experiences are subject to immediate recall and verbalization even though they are not in the center of consciousness at the time.

The Dynamic Unconscious

The concept of the *unconscious* presents much greater difficulties. How can we acquire knowledge about something which *by definition* is hidden? The unconscious is characterized by feelings, associations, wishes, strivings, etc. which are *actively* kept from entering the person's awareness. They are held back, as it were, by a dynamic force which insures the *status quo,* that is, they are *repressed.* Any attempt at bringing them into awareness is met by a *resistance* which is the operational manifestation of a *defense.* Repression, which results in total exclusion of an idea or feeling from awareness, is the prototype of all defenses. Repressions can only be inferred from the resisting force which opposes their becoming aware: they are never directly observable. It is therefore apparent that both the repressed material and the repressing force are unconscious. The repressing force may be viewed as a wall erected within the mental apparatus which prevents easy communication between the id and the ego. The superego often has a stake in maintaining this barrier, whose potential break-down or disintegration is subjectively experienced as a danger, to which the ego typically reacts with anxiety.

The Function of Repression

Let us take a somewhat closer look at repressions, their origin, and the reason for their coming into being. Freud started from the assumption (which more recently has been questioned) that at birth the human organism is "all id." It is governed by primitive impulses and strivings, rooted in its biological immaturity and consequent dependency upon nurturing adults. The ego at this time is either completely nonexistent or at any rate pitifully weak and ineffectual. The baby is almost completely at the mercy of his instinctual strivings over which he has virtually no control. Now as soon as a differentiation between the individual and the external world takes place (which is to say, as soon as a rudimentary ego develops), the child begins to exercise a measure of control over his inner impulses and strivings. He dimly perceives that some of his inner promptings are utterly incompatible with the expectations of the significant adults on whom he is dependent. That is, by giving these impulses full expression he would forfeit (so he fears) their love and incur their displeasure, or, what from the child's standpoint amounts to the same thing, he *fantasies* that other dire consequences will ensue unless his impulses are curbed. This distinction between reality and fantasy, however, is of the utmost importance as far as the child's subsequent development is concerned, and it invariably plays an important part in the maintenance and perpetuation of intrapsychic conflicts. At any rate, under the impact of real or imagined threats to the child's security, repressions come into being at a very early stage of his development. Probably a rudimentary (archaic) superego begins to function at about the same time. Henceforth "dangerous" impulses are walled off by a repressive counterforce and effectively removed from awareness or potential awareness. Repression contains and controls them and keeps them in check. Repression thus is the most primitive and the most powerful technique for removing "dangerous" impulses from awareness and denying their existence.

Repression is a most effective but also a potentially very dangerous defense. The danger lies in its permanence and immutability. Whereas mental contents which have not succumbed to the fate of repressions are subject to modification in the light of the person's accumulating life experience, repressed impulses never partake of *reality testing*. Both the impulse and the repressing force pertain to an early phase of the person's life and prove refractory to changed conditions. Yet the ego regards and deals with repressions as if they pertained to present-day reality. For example, a person may have repressed violent rage, fearing that its expression would destroy and utterly annihilate the person against whom it is directed (usually the parents of early childhood). In turn, because of the vehemence of the affect, the person has feared cruel and sadistic retribution from the attacked persons. Once the rage has been repressed, the issue is so to speak "closed." The person thus never has the opportunity of measuring his feelings against reality, and his mature ego continues to react to the original impulse (which is hidden from it) as did his infantile ego, which was weak, vulnerable, and greatly dependent upon the love and good-will of the significant adults.

This is the reason that repressed contents which include to a significant extent intense affects like rage, murderous wishes, and inordinate infantile demands for gratifications of various kinds, cannibalistic fantasies as well as primitive erotic feelings which were once experienced as incestuous, seem so horrendously dangerous to the ego. They are like skeletons in a closet which must never be opened lest—and this is the crux—the ego become totally overwhelmed by them, which would be tantamount to complete disintegration of the personality. The terror surrounding the possible breakthrough of such impulses into awareness is extremely difficult to appreciate by the average adult person, yet clinical observation abundantly demonstrates that the unraveling of an important repression can be one of the most frightening experiences a person can undergo.

Here we approach from a somewhat different vantage point the task of psychoanalysis and psychotherapy, which attempt to create conditions by which repressions can be undone. If this is successfully accomplished, the result is a strengthening of the adult ego and an increment in maturation. The objective is to convince the patient's adult ego that the dangerous situations from which it shrinks back are no longer so threatening as they once were when the patient was a child. With the help of the therapist who functions as the patient's auxiliary ego it then becomes possible, as the resistances are worked through, to lift repressions and thus to effect freer communication between the patient's ego and id.

Repressions, it is to be noted, are present in each and everyone of us. Like dikes, they are useful and indeed necessary for survival. It is only when they begin to interfere seriously with the person's psychological functioning and his adaptation to reality that they can become a serious problem. We shall see later how repressions and other defense mechanisms may create problems which require the intervention of the psychotherapist.

Anxiety

Anxiety is probably the most common symptom of neurosis. In contrast to fear, which usually refers to some external danger (like being attacked by a ferocious animal), anxiety is more mysterious because its source and origin are hidden from the person. Furthermore, while fear abates when the danger disappears, the same is often not true of anxiety. Anxiety may persist and be an almost ever-present emotion. As everyone knows from personal experience, it is extremely unpleasant and painful. At times anxiety becomes attached to an object in the external world, manifesting itself as an irrational fear, commonly called *phobia;* at other times it may be vague (free-floating). A person may have a phobia about speaking in public; being in an open or enclosed place; he may fear knives; snakes, or a host of other objects. It helps little to tell oneself that the object or the situation is really not dangerous — the anxiety persists. The writer knew a young woman who was deathly afraid of thunderstorms. Every morning she carefully listened to the weather report and scanned the sky for the slightest sign of a storm. When a thunderstorm did occur, she felt safe only when someone was with her; otherwise she crawled under a bed or hid in a corner of her apartment.

Irrational fears, as all parents know, are quite common in children, and they often have the appearance of a phobia. A child may be afraid of dogs although he may never have been bitten. Equally commonly, many childhood fears are eventually outgrown. Full-blown phobias, in adult life, on the other hand, are not so easily overcome.

Originally, Freud viewed anxiety as the result of repressed sexual energy (libido). In other words, if libido was "dammed up," it became converted into anxiety. This theory gradually proved unsatisfactory and was replaced in 1926 *(The Problem of Anxiety).* According to the new theory, which is still accepted, anxiety serves the function of a signal to inform the person that repressed feelings or impulses threaten to come to awareness. Thus, anxiety is a function of the ego which the latter employs to make sure that material once repressed remains in that state. According to this theory, anxiety came into being in childhood when the ego was weak and felt threatened by erotic or aggressive impulses arising from the id. Anxiety thus led to repression. Later on, whenever the "dangerous" situation recurs, anxiety signals a state of helplessness, or, more correctly, an anticipated state of helplessness. The ego, in effect, says: "I am afraid of being overwhelmed by impulses which I am utterly unable to handle." These impulses are so strong and appear so threatening that they may lead to complete disintegration of the personality.

Typical examples of early inner dangers are: birth, separation from the mother, loss of the penis, and loss of love—either of a person or one's superego.

How can anxiety be overcome? Basically, the approach is to force the ego to come face-to-face, as it were, with the threatening impulses and to demonstrate that they are not so dangerous as the ego had originally believed, and that the adult ego has the strength to control them. The threatening impulse, as Freud demonstrated, regularly represents a primitive wish—sexual or aggressive—and the situation which triggers the anxiety signal somehow provides an invitation for yielding to the wish. A man who develops keen anxiety when being alone with a woman is not afraid of adult sexual feelings toward another adult, but he develops anxiety because the situation reminds him of wishes and impulses he once had toward his mother when he was alone with her. Not uncommonly, sexual impulses are intertwined with angry and aggressive ones, not only toward the woman in this case, but more importantly perhaps toward the father (and toward the superego), both of whom are seen as sternly disapproving of the wish. The ego reacts with anxiety because it needs to control but fears it cannot, and besides it is tempted to make common cause with the id impulses, all of which tend to heighten the inner danger. In short, the ego reacts as if it can neither control nor reject the impulse that is pressing for awareness and ultimately, of course, action.

This example clearly illustrates one of the central aspects of any neurosis: The person, for reasons not known to him, misidentifies a situation in the present and reacts to it as he once did as a child. He confuses present-day reality with past reality, and past reality is often distorted in terms of the child's fantasies. Consequently, it is often less important what the parents actually said or did than what the child understood (or misunderstood). If we keep in mind the child's primitive impulses, his immaturity, and the vividness of his fantasy life, it is easy to see how gross misunderstandings and misinterpretations of reality can occur.

Manifestations of the Id

To return to the starting point of our discussion—the character of the mental qualities and the concept of the dynamic unconscious in particular—we must emphasize that by far the largest segment of the id is forever barred from consciousness. Freud likened the mental apparatus to an iceberg, large portions of which are completely submerged and only a fraction of which is ever visible. In a different metaphor, Freud has described the id as a "cauldron of seething emotions," many of which being contradictory, in a constant state of flux, vying with each other for expression (discharge), and creating tensions within the person. They are the raw materials and the source of energy of all mental acts.

Well, the reader may ask, if the id is unconscious and consequently unknowable, how can we find out about its functioning, its contents, and characteristics? True, little can be learned by studying the "normal" adult personality in its waking state. However, there are two conditions which provide limited access to the forces of the id. Both capitalize on the fact that id forces continually seek expression although, because of the restraining forces within the mental apparatus, such expressions are always indirect and partial. The two conditions are (1) either a weakening of the repressive forces or (2) an increase in the strength of the id forces seeking expression. Condition (1) occurs whenever the vigilance of the controlling ego is reduced. This takes place most commonly whenever the individual becomes drowsy, is about to fall asleep, or is actually asleep. It may occur, too, under the influence of alcohol or certain drugs, during hypnosis, in delirious states, and the like. Finally, the basic rule of free association in psychoanalytic therapy deliberately attempts to produce a reduction in the ego's watchfulness. Condition (2) is most commonly observed when repressions operating on a large scale and often in conflict with each other prevent over an extended period of time the expression of instintcual strivings. Enforced sexual abstinence is one such condition, but more common are severe neurotic conflicts. Parenthetically, we see here that a chronic "damming up" of instinctual impulses is a concomitant of neurotic disturbances; conversely, in the healthy personality there must be opportunities for a reasonable expression of instinctual strivings which "drain" a part of the id of accumulating energies.

The foregoing exposition may bear too much the earmarks of a hydraulic system—a charge that has been leveled against Freud in respect of his conception of the psychic apparatus and its energy distribution. Be that as it may. The point to be made is that (1) the id exerts a continuous influence over our mental life, suffusing as it does every mental act, albeit frequently in almost unrecognizable form, and (2) this influence is demonstrable under certain conditions. This recognition led Freud early in his career to an exhaustive study of the phenomena of dreaming, slips of the tongue, momentary forgetting, etc., which previously had been treated as trivia not worthy of the attention of a scientist. Freud's treatise on dreams, first published in 1900, is not only a brilliant monograph of his researches into a hitherto poorly understood area, but it is of tremendous theoretical significance in psychoanalysis, for here Freud gave a concise exposition of the dynamics of mental functioning. The book has remained one of the classics to which all students of psychoanalysis turn. Freud himself regarded it as his most original work, containing insights which, he felt, are vouchsafed to mortals only once in a lifetime. His inquiries into the phenomena of dreaming, in which he drew heavily on self-observations which he reported with courageous candor, demonstrated not only the *continuity of mental life* in all its phases but also the identity of psychic mechanisms which are at work in the formation of dreams as well as in the production of neurotic symptoms. A dream is the compromise solution of a neurotic conflict in miniature, just as a neurotic symptom is a compromise solution of a neurotic conflict on a larger scale. The psychic processes at work in both situations are qualititively indistinguishable.

This insight was a stroke of genius which launched Freud on the road of constructing a theoretical system of mental functioning which not only would account for psychopathological processes but of mental functioning in the healthy person as well. It will facilitate our approach to the understanding of intrapsychic conflict if, following Freud, we shall take a brief and relatively nontechnical look at the dynamics of dream formation.

CHAPTER **5**

The Psychodynamics
of Dreams

The study of dreams led Freud to a distinction between two principles of mental function, which he termed respectively the *primary* and the *secondary* process. This discovery has implications of the greatest importance and constitutes one of the cornerstones of the edifice of Freudian psychology. In several places this distinction has already been adumbrated, but further clarification is now in order.

In studying the mental processes of patients in psychoanalysis as well as through self-observation, Freud came to the conclusion that processes in the unconscious or the id are governed by laws which are entirely different from those in the preconscious or conscious ego. The id, as has already been pointed out, is conceived of as a nether world in which violent and intense impulses (wishes) hold sway. They are oblivious to the demands of reality, the rights of others, and, for that matter, very often to the welfare of the individual living in a complex world. These impulses are partly inborn, i.e., constitutionally determined; they are also part and parcel of the person's biological maturation. In energy terms, Freud viewed these impulses as charges (*cathexes*) which continually seek expression through the motor apparatus. Being uninfluenced by reality considerations, these cathexes are conceptualized as "mobile." Mobile cathexes, which are the essence of the

primary process, express themselves principally through *conden-*
sation and *symbolization*. Dream images typically are "carriers"
of primary process impulses which, in highly distorted form are
represented in the manifest content of dreams. According to Freud,
"No" does not exist in the id — only strivings seeking discharge.
Irrespective of their character, they are totally "blind" and often
utterly irrational. These wishes are the psychological counterpart
of instinctual energies which fuel the human organism's mental
functioning. While all dreams, in Freudian psychology, are viewed
as wish fulfillments, the term "wish," as we noted earlier, has a
very different meaning from the commonsense term which has
usually pleasant connotations. An unconscious wish originating in
the id, on the other hand, may not at all be experienced as pleasant
by the person's ego; in fact, it often has a decidedly unpleasant,
painful, and often repugnant quality. This explains the apparent
contradiction between the notion of a dream as wish—fulfillment
and anxiety dreams: Anxiety arises when the dreamer becomes
dimly aware of a "wish" that is unacceptable to his ego or superego.

Condensation, Displacement, and Symbolization

Condensation refers to the fact that any dream image is a
highly compressed, meager, and laconic expression of an important
problem the dreamer is working over. As Freud points out, a
dream is not a faithful translation of the underlying dream thought,
but the dream thought itself has undergone considerable transfor-
mation before it results in the image that we remember upon
awakening. Another important aspect of the process of condensation is what Freud calls the *overdetermined* character of any
dream image. A person, object, or event occurring in a dream never
has a single meaning; rather the meaning represents a convergence
of a wide variety of thoughts, feelings, memories, etc., many of
which are highly personal to the dreamer. Nor is a dream image
ever random or haphazard; instead, it constitutes a focal point for
the problem with which the dream, unbeknown to the dreamer,
attempts to deal. A corner in the living room of one's childhood
home, a landmark on the way to school, the bathing of a sibling—
to name but a few examples—conjure up a host of associations in
the mind of anyone. Similarly, the dream image brings together
in highly abbreviated (condensed) form a wide range of meanings.
The same, we may note parenthetically, is true of a neurotic symp-

tom, like in irrational fear. The feared object has many meanings to the patient, most of which he does not properly understand on a conscious level. But it can be understood if we learn to decipher the language of the unconscious and the particular laws it obeys. Freud gives many examples to illustrate these points.

From studying his own dreams and those of his patients, it also became evident to Freud that often the very essence of a dream is not represented in the dream. What may be of the greatest interest to the dreamer may appear in the dream as a trivial detail or it may be completely "forgotten." What has happened is a *displacement*—from the important to the trivial, from one image to another, and the like. The reason for this occurrence is to be found in the censorship which any dream must overcome. An un-invited guest may not be able to get by the doorman, but if he comes disguised as an important personage he may gain ready admittance. In dreams the reverse is often true. A conflict of the dreamer, if represented directly in the dream, would never get past the censor; but if it appears in the guise of a trivial detail, it may circumvent the "watchman."

Thus, condensation and displacement are the governing factors which are responsible for the particular form a dream takes.

Finally, we must take note of the manner in which dream images are represented. The idea of dream symbols is common enough, and innumerable dream books supply the supposed meaning of an object or action occurring in a dream. True, Freud also recognized some universal symbols, particularly those pertaining to masculinity (sharp, pointed objects) and femininity (hollow, vessel-like objects), but by and large the individual, personal meaning of dream symbols is not readily apparent. The process of *symbolization* is well illustrated in the following example reported by Freud:

> One of my patients, a man whose sexual abstinence was imposed on him by a severe neurosis, and whose [unconscious] phantasies were fixed upon his mother, had repeated dreams of going upstairs in her company. I once remarked to him that a moderate amount of masturbation would probably do him less harm than his compulsive self-restraint, and this provoked the following dream:
>
> *His piano-teacher reproached him for neglecting his piano-playing, and for not practicing Moscheles' 'Etudes' and Clementi's 'Gradus ad Parnassum.'*

By way of comment, he pointed out that *'Gradus'* are also 'steps' and that the key-board itself is a staircase, since it contains scales [ladders].

It is fair to say that there is no group of ideas that is incapable of representing sexual facts and wishes.

The Interpretation of Dreams, p. 371-372.

Primary and Secondary Process

The principles governing the *primary* process are diametrically opposed to rational, reasonable, reality-oriented, adaptational ones which are characteristic of the *secondary* process which governs the ego. The latter, to repeat, is always concerned with the person's relationships with the external world, with adaptation, and "fitting in." The ego, through the secondary process, observes the laws of reason and logic, delays instinctual gratification or brings about conditions under which safe gratification is possible, assesses the consequences of the person's actions, and, if necessary, suppresses altogether the expression of instinctual impulses.

It may be seen that the superego plays an important part in judging the performance of the ego: It may "smile benevolently" upon the ego's activities or criticize them sharply if the superego's standards and requirements are not met. A well-functioning, psychologically healthy person is one in whom the three agencies of the psychic apparatus live in relative harmony: the ego provides a certain amount of gratification for the impulses emanating from the id, and the superego accepts the ego's overall performance as meeting its standards. Neurotic disturbances are situations in which the person has failed to arrive at a *modus vivendi* between id, ego, and superego, and where internecine war rather than harmony prevails.

The Dream-work: Further Comments

The easiest and most readily observed manifestations of these two processes occur in the process of dreaming, with which every-one is familiar. Freud made a distinction between the *manifest* and the *latent* content of the dream, and laid special emphasis on the *dream-work* which produces the grotesque distortions so character-istic of dream productions. What one recalls of a dream upon awakening constitutes the manifest content. The latent content, as in Joseph's interpretations of Pharaoh's dream, represents the underlying meaning. Dreams are always concerned with some problem or concern of the dreamer; they are completely egocentric; and they are always linked to an event, association, or memory pertaining to the previous day (*day residue*). The most important aspect of the dream, as Freud demonstrated, is neither the manifest nor the latent content of the dream, but rather the dream-work, that is, the process by which the dreamer produces the strange mental product of the dream, which has occupied the interest of mankind from the dawn of history. Dreams which previously were seen as inspirations by God or the Devil, or as prophetic messages from another world, were now conceived of as natural functions of the human mind.

According to Freud's conception, a dream, like a neurotic symptom, represents a *compromise* between a wish seeking expression (always ultimately for the purpose of seeking discharge through motor action) and the desire for sleep. The possibility for dreaming is provided by the ego's diminished vigilance over impulses during sleeping. At such a time an id impulse seeking discharge attempts to force its way into the ego or, a memory from the preceding day somehow activitates an unconscious impulse with which it makes a connection. In his early writings Freud spoke of a "censor" inherent in the ego which, comparable to a watchman, insures that unwelcome impulses are kept under repression. This controlling process is most effective during the waking state, but is reduced as soon as the person has gone to sleep and the possibility for expression through the motor apparatus (skeletal musculature) has been abolished. But even during deep sleep, the ego does not completely abandon its watchfulness, and impulses emanating from the id must disguise themselves, as it were, to "get by" the ego's barriers. These disguises are effected, as we have stated, through such maneuvers as *displacement, condensation,* and *symbolization.*

The impulses emanating from the id always originate in and are characteristic of the patient's childhood. Thus, they necessarily have a thoroughly infantile and primitive character, which is the reason that any dream, properly interpreted, can be seen as the expression of an infantile wish or striving. While dreaming, the person reverts (*regresses*) to early periods of his life. But, the important point is that these impulses never appear in *direct* form, which would be too threatening to the ego whose concern is the maintenance of sleep. They are always disguised and distorted.

The process by which these distortions are produced constitutes the heart of the dream-work.

A dream can be adequately interpreted only by recourse to the associations of the dreamer to the various dream elements. In other words, in order to understand a dream, it is usually necessary to know a great deal about the dreamer, his current life and life problems, the events of the previous days which provided the stimulus for the dream, and the memories which are recalled in free association. Even then there will be dreams which defy understanding. While every dream is potentially interpretable, this is not always true in actuality. Certainly, it cannot be understood by reference to the popular "dream books," in which objects have invariant meanings. Freud approached the analysis of dreams by asking the dreamer (often himself) to report his associations to each and every element of the dream. Sometimes he found that aspects of the dreams which appeared clearest in the dreamer's recall were not the most important ones (another form of disguise). Another aid in dream interpretation consists of asking the person to report the same dream twice. Such accounts are often not identical, even when told in immediate succession, but elements omitted from the first account may occur in the second and thus provide relevant clues. Even the conscious recall of a dream is often a further distortion of what has actually been dreamed.

Summary

The essence of the dream, then, is the emergence of an id impulse which seeks gratification through discharge. Direct discharge being blocked due to the unacceptability of the infantile impulse to the conscious ego (because it would produce conflict with the superego or the external world and thus endanger the individual), the impulse, as it were, hoodwinks the somnolent ego by using various disguises to express itself. The expression takes place by means of a hallucinatory experience in which id impulses use available memory traces to force their way through to awareness. The memory traces may be viewed as the carriers to which the impulse attaches itself, which it influences, and—in a way—"bribes." If the disguise is successful the person continues sleeping. If the ego detects the true nature of the impulse, experiences it as too threatening, and thus needs to reject it, the dreamer experiences anxiety and wakes up.

A dream is always concerned with a problem of the dreamer; it is never an idle preoccupation. Moreover, it is an attempt to produce a solution to the problem. Since a dream provides at least a partial discharge of the id impulse, it plays an important part in the psychic economy of the person and serves a salutary function. Through dreaming the person discharges tensions (often the counterpart of unconscious wishes) in a harmless way. Recent research on dreaming, for example, has shown that when a person is regularly awakened whenever he is dreaming (a technique for detecting dreams through eye movements has been developed in recent years) and this process is continued for several nights, he becomes exceedingly irritable, frustrated, and restless. To deprive a person of the opportunity to dream, therefore, is to deprive him of an important avenue for the expression of instinctual impulses. Dreams are a necessity of psychic life.

CHAPTER 6

The Neurotic Conflict

As we have seen in the preceding chapter, dreams are made of the same cloth as neurotic symptoms and obey the same psychological laws as a full-blown neurosis. Nevertheless, a dream is usually a transient phenomenon and a miniature edition of a psychic conflict. We need to achieve greater clarity concerning the dynamics and the origin (*etiology*) of intrapsychic conflicts, for psychoanalysis, both in its theoretical postulates as well as in its therapeutic objectives is a psychology of conflict. How does an intrapsychic conflict come to play such a major part in a person's mental health, how does it come into being, how is it perpetuated, how does it give rise to anguish and suffering, and how does it eventually become amenable to resolution? These, after all, are questions which lie at the core of Freudian psychology.

Origins in Childhood

Freud asserted categorically that the origin of a neurotic conflict is always to be sought in the person's early childhood. He admitted one notable exception, the "traumatic neuroses," which occur as a result of intense emotional upheavals, as for example among soldiers during wartime. But even here we must assume the existence of latent conflicts which have their roots in childhood and which become activated under unusually stressful life situations. Furthermore, the formation of a neurotic conflict, which

47

gives rise to troublesome neurotic symptoms in adulthood or adolescence, presupposes a weak ego, a condition which is characteristic of early emotional development. A neurotic disturbance is essentially an ego weakness, an intrapsychic dilemma, if you will. The ego, unable to withstand the onsloughts of instinctual impulses from within and environmental pressures from without, has arrived at a compromise solution, which while seemingly successful at the time, has proven an obstacle to the person's adaptation to life. In order to lend greater concreteness to such abstract statements, we need to remind ourselves once again of the circumstances in which the growing child finds himself.

As we have repeatedly pointed out, Freud regarded the small child as being largely dominated by instinctual forces which impel him to seek gratification from the significant adults in his environment. He is governed by the "pleasure principle," that is, a blind seeking for tension reduction through the discharge of his instinctual strivings. This seeking for discharge at first has little regard for reality, the rights of others, the limitations of parents, and their inability perpetually to guarantee a tensionless state in the child. (Sleep, we might note, is the prototype of such complete "happiness," as far as the infant is concerned, and even for the adult, sleep regularly serves the all-important function of complete withdrawal from the problems, demands, duties, and responsibilities of the external world.) From the child's point of view, everything that conduces to his gratification is "good" and everything that imposes frustration and deprivation is "evil" or "bad." He comes to value significant adults in the same terms, so that the mother (or earlier, her nipple as a "part object") is "good" to the extent that she gratifies the child's wishes, and she is "bad" to the extent that she imposes frustrations. Similarly, the child's impulses which are gratified by the nurturing adults are experienced as "good", and angry, hostile, destructive feelings which are met with disapproval from the outside world are felt as "bad." In this way, too, the child comes to value himself as "good" or "bad" depending on the manner in which his instinctual needs are treated by others. Thus, self-esteem is deeply rooted in the child's earliest experiences of gratification (or contrariwise, frustration). Object-seeking instinctual strivings were characterized by Freud as *sexual* or *psychosexual* in a broad sense (Eros). Hostile, angry, destructive impulses, with which everyone is endowed, were seen in Freud's later formulations as manifestations of the death instinct (Thanatos).

The latter instinct, it must be pointed out, has remained a controversial concept within psychoanalytic theory.

Attempted Solutions and Failures

The child's budding ego, we have also observed, is at first a very weak structure and no equal to the imperious drives which seek continual expression through discharge. Given benevolent and affectionate parental guidance, the ego manages eventually to achieve increasing control over these impulses. Thus they become bound and channeled, serving the individual in his increasing adaptation to the external world. The goal of growing up, according to this conception, is the development of a strong ego (executive apparatus) which mediates effectively between (1) the inner strivings, (2) the demands of the external world, and (3) the dictates of the superego, which represents the precipitates of the teachings, prohibitions, injunctions, etc. imposed by parental authority. As the superego gains in strength, it is no longer the beloved parents whose displeasure is incurred when their dictates are disobeyed, but the child himself takes over this rewarding and punishing function. The child thus becomes increasingly independent and self-regulating. If the parental authority was for the most part reasonable, mild, and just, the child begins to look at himself in the same light. Contrariwise, harsh, oppressive, dictatorial, and tyrannical attitudes of the parents are similarly built into the superego, and become the child's own attitude toward himself.

The child's mental apparatus is shaped both by inner instinctual strivings (which in turn have their roots in his heredity, temperament, and biological equipment) as well as by external influences, as represented by the parents or their surrogates. This point is crucial because it stresses the fact that Freudian psychology is neither entirely on the "nature" side nor is it entirely on the "nurture" side of the time-honored controversy. Interestingly, Freud has been accused by some critics of stressing biological (instinctual) factors at the expense of socioenvironmental influences, and by others of the opposite. A careful reading of his writings shows that he never neglected the psychological influences of the parents as mediators of the culture within which the child grows up, and the influence of his basic biological orientation on all his writings is self-evident.

The central point is that the ego is on the one hand at the mercy of powerful forces from within as well as from without, and it is the child's job, from a very early age on, to find a *modus vivendi* between these two poles. To resolve the dilemma, only a limited number of avenues are open to the ego. Essentially, they are of two kinds. Either the ego modifies itself (called an *autoplastic* solution) or it can modify the external environment (called an *alloplastic* solution). The situation is not unlike that of an employee who has a disagreeable boss. How can he cope with his predicament? First, he can exclude the entire problem from awareness and convince himself that it does not exist. This is roughly analogous to repression. Second, he can try to change himself so that the troublesome situation becomes more pleasant. This, in fact, is the solution most commonly employed by the small child. The trouble with this accommodation is that the boss may *really* be a querulous fellow, and if the employee is able to assess the situation accurately—which the small child because of his immaturity is not able to do—he might find that it is not worth the trouble to change himself, and that indeed it may be harmful to modify his personality simply to get along. The third possibility is to try to change the boss, by manipulating him or by working out a tolerable relationship. To some extent, most children succeed in this solution. The fourth technique would be to leave the bad situation altogether. This road, for obvious reasons, is closed to the child. Many adults, it may be noted parenthetically, often employ the same infantile techniques that were available to them at an early period on their life and prefer to complain about a seemingly immutable situation rather than seeking ways and means of changing it. The "reward" for maintaining the status quo often is the perpetuation of a dependency relationship, which may be preferable unconsciously to the dangers and uncertainties of striking out on one's own.

We note here that the *genesis of neurotic disorders lies in the total life situation of the small child.* Neurosis is not a "disease," a "vice" or an illness in the medical sense; rather it is the outcome of a faulty educational process which rarely can (or for that matter, should) be "blamed" on anyone. Parents usually make the mistakes they make out of ignorance or because of their own neurotic problems rather than with "malice aforethought" or out of sheer viciousness.

A neurotic conflict, then, is a failure on the part of the growing ego to work out viable solutions to the adaptational problems confronting it. This failure results in various distortions of the ego itself and the formation of neurotic symptoms, which are the most easily recognizable form in which underlying intrapsychic conflicts manifest themselves. We shall next examine how the ego manages to "produce" symptoms.

As Freud viewed the position of the weak ego, its tendency is to "shrink back" from the instinctual demands which it feels powerless to contain, and, what amounts to the same thing, which (subjectively) threaten to overwhelm it. The most radical measure which the ego employs to stem the tide is to repress the unwelcome instinctual demand, to treat it as an alien intruder which it will not tolerate. A counterforce thus becomes pitted against the id impulse (technically termed a *anti-cathexis*). This "solution" is effective as long as the counter-charge remains equal to the impulse striving for expression. Many impulses in the healthy personality are thus permanently banned from awareness, but at the expense of being excluded from the development of the total personality. It is as if the ego had slammed the door against a dimly perceived threatening intruder, but once the door has been shut the ego will never know whether the intruder was indeed as threatening as he was believed to be, or, whether it is worth spending energy in keeping him out. If, as Freud believed, the mental apparatus operates with a fixed amount of psychic energy (the *constancy principle*), repressions commit a certain portion of this available energy to a particular function. Once this energy is used for repressive purposes, it cannot be used as "free" energy in the task of adaptation. The ego to this extent has become inhibited in its functioning and has placed restrictions upon itself. The *quantitative* factor here, as elsewhere in the psychic economy, is of the essence: the question is how much energy is committed in repression and how much is freely available. In extreme cases, the ego's function may become so restricted as to lead to complete mental paralysis. In other words, the person may be so inhibited that he has little energy available to relate to other people and to master life.

It is also apparent that while in the case of repression the instinctual impulse is held in check, this does not diminish its energy. Stated otherwise, while barred from expression, the impulse continually "presses upward" and seeks channels of discharge. As we have seen, one devious route which this process sometimes takes is via a dream. In this case, it may bypass the repression and become fused with a preconscious impulse, which in turn may find its way into consciousness. But here only a partial discharge of the energy occurs.

Repression has another adverse consequence. The ego continues to react to the instinctual impulse as a threatening event despite the ego's lessened vulnerability. That is, the ego behaves vis-á-vis the impulse as if it were weak and vulnerable as it was in childhood when the repression came into being. Ordinarily the ego's perception of the external world undergoes change in accordance with the maturation of the organism. However, the ego is "blind" as far as the inner strivings are concerned against which it defends itself. The ego's reaction to such impulses thus is thoroughly infantile, and any attempt at undoing an existing repression is met with the signal of anxiety. It is for this reason that in analytic therapy, one of whose major tasks is the undoing of repression, the ego defends itself against the therapist who attempts to undo the repression as if its survival depended on it. In short, it is extraordinarily difficult to convince the ego that the danger which it fears so vividly is out of all proportion to the reality of the situation.

The Defenses

Repression, as we noted previously, is the prototype of all defenses. It is complete and radical. As the person matures, other kinds of defenses are used with greater frequency. Anna Freud, the renowned daughter of the founder of psychoanalysis, carefully worked out the mechanisms by which the ego defends itself against unwanted impulses. Defenses always are mechanisms of the ego by which unwelcome instinctual impulses are rendered less threatening.

Projection, for example, consists in attributing an instinctual striving to the outside world. Thus, a hostile impulse which originates within the person is attributed to another individual. Consequently, the formula is no longer: I hate him, but he hates me. On this supposition (which the ego tends to accept as a truth), it then becomes necessary to defend oneself against the alleged hostility of the person by aggression and similar techniques. Of course, the more another person is imbued with hateful impulses, the more it is necessary to be on guard oneself and to fear the other's person's attacks. The suspiciousness of the *paranoid* person is thus a result of the projection of his hostile impulses into the outside world. Projection, like all defenses, serves an adaptive function because in some sense it is easier for the ego to cope with an outside danger than with a threat from within. By the same token, a phobia serves to change a fear of one's inner impulses into an outside danger, from which—at least in principle—one can escape. The trouble is that this unconscious technique often has its own built-in problems.

Reaction formation is another defense mechanism which is universally used—always unconsciously, it goes without saying. An individual who believes he has to disown powerful sadistic impulses which are ego-alien turns them into their opposite: he becomes meek, compliant, and submissive. A fearful person disguises his fears by a show of bravado, and may even excel through courage and gallantry.

Psychoanalysis distinguishes several additional defense mechanisms, all of which represent unconscious techniques employed by the ego to fend off unwelcome instinctual strivings. The defensive structure is typically a complicated network, with several defenses working in conjunction to achieve the main objective. It is a common finding that defenses call for the development of additional defenses to make the original one "safer." Thus, the original impulse is extraordinarily well disguised, and often identifiable only after a very considerable amount of therapeutic work has been accomplished. The motive force fueling any defense is the *avoidance of pain;* conversely, defenses first come into being to terminate a painful situation.

Mention should be made of another defense which Freud regarded as the most desirable unconscious technique for dealing with instinctual impulses. This is *sublimation.* In this defense mechanism—it may not be a defense in the strict sense at all— the ego succeeds in neutralizing an instinctual drive, largely robbing it of its primitive character and turning it into an activity which, while providing a measure of instinctual gratification, is socially acceptable. Many human activities are of this type. For example, a surgeon may discharge through his professional activity some of his sadistic impulses, or a painter may satisfy anal strivings by working with oils and paints. Such activities are fully acceptable to all parts of the person's mental apparatus (*ego-syntonic*) and no longer involve a recognizable intrapsychic conflict.

Complications often arise because the superego "takes sides" in the conflict. On the one hand, it influences the ego by disapproval lest it curb the id impulse; on the other hand, it may make common cause with the id and "take over" the latter's erotic and aggressive strivings, which again it directs against the ego. This situation often prevails in the process of symptom formation. The syptomatic act (whether it be a compulsion to wash one's hands, to avoid particular situations such as heights, enclosed places, fainting spells, etc.) permits a disguised expression of the impulse which is unacceptable to the ego. The latter, as it were, permits an act which gives the appearance of being innocuous, while at the same time it represses its full energy charge. Interestingly, the symptomatic act, no matter how well disguised it may appear, usually contains an element of the original impulse which it seeks to contain. Thus, as Freud observed, the symptom reveals a "return of the repressed."

Symptoms are frequently exceedingly complicated psychic structures in that they represent a confluence of several impulses and defending forces. They are, in Freud's term, *"overdetermined."* In fact, there is rarely a simple cause-and-effect relationship, and overdetermination is the rule rather than the exception. Furthermore, symptoms are embedded in, and the product of, the person's character structure. Just as a person whose respiratory system represents the "weak spot" of his physical constitution is likely to contract pneumonia, whereas another person, differently disposed, is more likely to develop gastrointestinal symptoms during an influenza epidemic, so a given neurotic symptom is more likely to occur in a person with a particular personality structure which predisposes him to this particular development. Moreover, as has already been hinted at, the person's character structure, by which is meant his enduring personality trends, typically is itself a resultant of conflicts with which the ego has struggled at a crucial developmental phase. Submissiveness, timidity, aggressiveness, etc. are examples of characterological trends which represent fusions of conflicting instinctual tendencies with ego forces.

The Oedipus Complex

Freud stated that "the weak point in the organization of the ego lies in its behavior toward the sexual function, as though the biological opposition between self-preservation and the preservation of the species there found psychological expression" (*Outline*, p. 87). He further believed that no single set of factors was of such crucial importance in the formation of neurotic conflicts as well as the person's personality structure as the Oedipus complex. The complex is usually defined as the little boy's desire to marry his mother and to kill his father as the rival for the mother's affection. The female version of the conflict is occasionally referred to as Electra complex. Neither statement is particularly meaningful to the general reader. The difficulty lies in the schematic presentations which are often given of the childhood situation in which these complexes have their origin. Also, in analytic work one rarely finds the Oedipus complex (the term is generally preferred in describing the conflict for both sexes) in exactly this form. It may be instructive to take a look, once again, at the position of the developing child vis-á-vis his parents.

Clinical observations document the fact that every child develops both tender and hostile impulses toward the persons who are emotionally most significant for him, first the mother, and at a later age (about 3-4) the father. As reality becomes more clearly differentiated, he recognizes that the parents have lives of their own, that their sole raison d'être is not to serve him and to gratify all his wishes, and that he is faced with the necessity of scaling down his demands and to fit to the structure of the family in his role as a child. Often he may find that he has to compete with siblings for the parents' attention, and even if he is an only child the parents ration their nurturing activities toward him and pursue interests of their own. The first blow (trauma) to his self-centeredness which every child has to master is an increasing separation from the mother. At first, the child lives in a state of close union (*symbosis*) with the mother. Only gradually—very gradually— he comes to see himself as an individual in his own right. Depending on the quality of the mother-child relationship, this separation can be an extremely painful process (particularly if the child experiences it as a rejection). In the majority of circumstances, fortunately, the problem is mastered with relative ease. However, separation and loss loom as a dangerous "complex" in the unconscious of everyone.

"The Little Boy's Dilemma"

As time goes on, the little boy develops highly affectionate and erotically tinged feelings toward his mother. These feelings are a composite of dependency needs, erotic feelings, and at times frankly sexual ones. Thus he comes to experience the father as a rival for the mother's affection and he becomes keenly competitive with him. However, usually he also has strong affectionate feelings toward his father, with which the competitive and rivalrous feelings come into conflict. Depending on many factors, these competitive feelings may reach great intensity and include death wishes as well as other destructive fantasies toward the father. As a result, the boy will fear retaliation from a male who is so much more powerful and competent than he. The most dire consequence the boy fears is that his father will deprive him of his penis (*castration anxiety*) which he has come to value, during the phallic phase of development, as a priceless possession. This fear, coupled with the wish to identify with his much admired father, eventually leads him to abandon his erotic interest in the mother. This, in psychological terms, is the price he must pay for the safeguarding of his own masculinity. By giving up his incestuous strivings toward the mother, he demonstrates his obedience to the authority of the father, and gains the right to grow up to become "like him." This identification also includes the promise to use his sexual prowess at a later stage in relation to a nonincestuous object. This resolution is never smooth and often gives rise to complications which become the nuclei of neurotic difficulties. For example, the boy, out of fear of his father, may identify with the mother, and assume a passive feminine role in relation to the father. Or, if the father is experienced by the boy as weak and ineffectual, or if he is completely absent by virtue of death or divorce, the boy fails to develop the necessary masculine identification and the superego controls which are a part of it. To take the mystery out of what may at first blush appear to be a fanciful account, we must remember that we are dealing with a variegated set of attitudes, feelings, and reaction tendencies which only for schematic purposes can be lumped under a shorthand label of "the Oedipus complex."

The substance of the conflictual situation is the early flowering of sexual feelings and fantasies which, qualitatively, are the same as in the adult, but which may prove to be extraordinarily threatening to the child because of his biological immaturity and his dependency upon the people toward whom these intense feelings are directed. Nor must we forget that some mothers, for neurotic reasons of their own, unwittingly encourage sexual feelings in their small sons, particularly when their marital relationship is problematic. They may thus look upon and unconsciously relate to the child as a substitute lover. Thus, on the one hand, the boy will feel pleasantly enticed by such unconscious seduction, but since in the final analysis there can be no consummation of this "romance" he will eventually be bitterly disappointed. As already indicated, the Oedipus situation also can become greatly complicated if the child has been traumatized during the earlier phases of his personality development. Again, the factors here are multitudinous; there is no single formula; and in each instance highly individual variables color the particular constellation. In all instances the significant experiences and feelings are thoroughly and rather deeply repressed. This is true both of the "normal" individual as well as the person who is destined to become psychologically disordered at a later stage in his life.

"The Little Girl's Dilemma"

In the case of the girl, the developmental sequence, as worked out by Freud, follows a different path. Again it must be remembered that we are dealing with a schematic presentation, which varies widely in each individual case. Like the boy, the girl at first forms a close affectionate tie with the mother. However, as she reaches the age of the Oedipal phase she makes the discovery that the mother (contrary to early infantile beliefs of both boys and girls) lacks a penis. The child, unaware of primary sex differences, from that point on regards the mother as "mutilated." That is, the girl believes that the mother (and she) once had a penis but that somehow she "lost" it. This, according to Freud, establishes a deeply ingrained sense of inferiority in every woman, as well as the desire to regain (what the girl fantasied as once having been) the *status quo ante*. She competes for the father's affection and begins to see the mother as a rival. Also, she blames the mother for the felt biological "deficiency" and directs her hatred against her. Furthermore, she wishes to obtain from the father what she felt was denied her by the mother. The wish for a penis gradually gives rise to a wish for a child from the father. But that wish, too, of course is frustrated. Typically, in the normal course of development, the girl eventually identifies with the mother despite her ambivalent feelings for her and more or less accepts her "inferior" role vis-á-vis the male: she becomes compliant and submissive, and in general accepts the feminine role. But while there is a "reward" for the boy for giving up his erotic interest in the mother, in the sense that in so doing he can identify with the powerful father and retain the hope of exercising his sexual powers at a later stage (that is, his penis is preserved), the girl, in these terms, must accept a "second best" solution. To be sure, she retains the hope of becoming like mother and eventually may hope to have a child of her own by a man other than the father, but she can rarely resolve the hostility against the mother for having "cheated" her. Clinical observation bears out Freud that many women continue into adulthood to entertain strong competitive strivings with men, whom they view as "superior" beings and whose "equal" they deeply feel they can never become (penis envy).

Freud regarded as the most basic problems in human psychology the man's tendency to assume a passive attitude toward other men, and the woman's desire for a penis. He also believed that human nature was intrinsically bisexual in a psychological sense, so that there are strong feminine strivings in every man and masculine strivings in every woman. In either case, the situation is always highly complex.

Summary

A neurotic conflict, according to Freud, is essentially an *unconscious* intrapsychic struggle between the ego and the id. It takes its origin from the childhood situation in which the ego was weak and vulnerable to strong instinctual striving from the id, which for the most part are sexual and aggressive in nature. Unable to channel, modify, or relinquish the strivings, the ego has resorted to pseudo-solutions which partly contain the impulse and, in the case of a frank neurotic symptom, permit it disguised expression. The basic struggle is always unconscious. Every person is prone to the formation of neurotic conflicts because of the early flowering of sexuality during the Oedipal period, and his ego may be predisposed to conflict by earlier painful experiences in relation to the significant adults of the person's childhood.

A neurotic conflict can be abolished by teaching the ego to accept, tolerate, and modify the subjectively threatening impulse, that is, by strengthening its executive powers.

CHAPTER **7**

Transference Neuroses
and Transference

Although Freud from the beginning was interested in helping
the patients who consulted him for their "nervous" disorders, he
soon came to realize that there was nothing wrong with their nerves
in a neurological sense. Furthermore, his desire to cure his patients
gradually was overshadowed by his desire to understand, from the
standpoint of the scientist, what ailed these people. For one thing,
he refused to regard his patients as peculiar, deviant, or deserving
of blame. This was an accomplishment in its own right. Secondly,
he found it necessary to invent concepts which would serve as
building blocks for a theory to understand the human mind and its
workings. These concepts were based upon, and had their roots in,
a wealth of observations which Freud was able to make in listening
to his patients for countless hours. The general reader, lacking this
clinical experience, often has difficulty in supplying the context to
understand more deeply the meaning of Freud's ideas and theoretical formulations. He listens to the words, many of which have
acquired colloquial meanings, but often he cannot relate them to
anything in his own experience. Thus, he may tend to reject Freud's
notions for personal or extraneous reasons. In may ways this attitude is comparable to the person who refuses to look through a
microscope because he "knows" what there is to be seen.

In any case, Freudian formulations are a serious effort to
describe and explain psychic phenomena as naturally occurring

events. Indeed, throughout his life, Freud was a sober, dispassionate, and unswervingly serious observer of man's behavior and motivations. He attempted to explain what he saw—not what a moralist might like to see. Above all, he accepted human behavior and motivations as meaningful and potentially capable of explanation, no matter how trivial, "strange," or even repulsive they might occasionally appear. His approach was that of the scientist who reports what he sees—no more, no less—and who tries to understand as best he can the phenomena he had set out to study. With respect to the vagaries of human behavior, this was a novelty in Freud's day and constitutes one important mark of his genius.

As has been suggested, Freud believed that in the complex process of growing up it is very difficult for anyone to escape neurotic conflicts. Whether a person "succeeds" (the quotation marks are intended to underscore the fact that developmental events are quite outside any person's volitional control) in repressing such conflicts, in surmounting them by one adaptational technique or another, or whether in adult life he succumbs to serious difficulties—is largely a question of a quantitative factor. This factor is made up of the person's heredity, his constitution, and the particular life experiences to which he was exposed in early childhood. Certainly it is true that later events may either alleviate early unhappy experiences or they may aggravate them, but the roots of neurotic difficulties are always to be found in early childhood. Thus, there is continuity and orderliness in the development of the human personality.

We must also remember that the neurotic difficulties which eventually bring a person to psychoanalysis or to some other form of psychological therapy are rarely isolated symtoms existing, as it were, as a foreign body in an otherwise healthy personality. Much more common is the situation in which neurotic symptoms are the foci of pervasive underlying difficulties forming an integral part of the individual's personality. True, in his early years Freud himself focused heavily on *symptoms* and their treatment, but eventually he came to recognize the crucial importance of the entirety of the individual's character structure. Indeed, many persons today enter psychotherapy without manifesting the "classical" symptoms of one or another form of neurosis. Their emotional difficulties may be vague feelings of discontent, unhappiness, tension, anxiety, and the like.

The Transference Neuroses

Freud originally maintained that psychoanalysis was the treatment of choice for the so-called *transference neuroses*, that it was inapplicable to the major psychoses in which the patient's orientation to reality is grossly disturbed, and of limited value in the kinds of characterological difficulties that have just been alluded to. The touchstone of this general classification was the extent to which the patient was able to form a working relationship with the therapist. In turn, this ability turned upon Freud's conception of the *transference,* which we shall presently consider in greater detail. The essence, however, was that the outlook for therapeutic improvement was commensurate with the patient's ability to transfer to the therapist (as a contemporary figure who stood *in loco parentes*) feelings and attitudes that pertained to early childhood, but which were still alive and found expression through his symptoms. In other words, therapy was seen as propitious if it succeeded in rolling back time and if the patient was able to revive in the present, conflicts he had with significant figures of his childhood. On the other hand, he believed that patients who had broken with reality, that is, persons suffering from the most serious mental disorders (*psychoses*), were unable to form such a relationship with the therapist, hence they could not be reached by psychoanalysis. For different reasons, he believed that similarly unfavorable circumstances obtained in many other conditions, which correspondingly were thought to be untreatable by psychoanalysis.

In more recent years it has been shown that even severely disturbed psychotic patients can be successfully treated with modified forms of psychotherapy, although at times this is an arduous and extremely protracted undertaking.* The strictures which Freud entertained with respect to characterological difficulties also seem to be not universally applicable. On the other hand, it should be pointed out that Freud never considered psychoanalysis (or, for that matter, psychotherapy) a panacea for man's emotional ills. In his claims he was considerably more cautious and reserved than some of his followers.

---

*The most serious but also the most common psychotic disorder is *schizophrenia*, which is often characterized by a disintegration of the personality, including disordered thinking. *Manic-depressive* psychosis, a disorder characterized by extreme mood swings, is another major psychosis.

Since the transference neuroses first engaged the interest of psychoanalysis, and since to this date they are the conditions for which psychoanalysis (or psychoanalytically oriented therapy) has remained the treatment of choice, it will be helpful to characterize them in somewhat greater detail. It must be noted at the outset that no neurotic condition is ever encountered in "pure form"; mixtures of symptom patterns are much more typical; and everyone, in the final analysis, represents a mixture of one of the basic "neurotic" types. While the system of classification which Freud used is no longer generally accepted, nevertheless whatever designation is chosen, the basic symptom pictures and personality constellations have remained remarkably stable.

The conditions which Freud thought especially amenable to therapy by psychoanalysis were hysteria, anxiety states, the phobias, and obsessive-compulsive disorders. Less suitable he considered so-called organic neuroses (which in the more recent past have found their place in the larger area of *psychosomatic conditions*), sexual perversions (particularly homosexuality), and *psychopathic states.** The major psychoses (schizophrenia in its various forms and manic-depressive psychosis, as already noted) were specifically excluded. It lies beyond the scope of this book to describe the psychological dynamics of the various disease entities (*syndromes*). The interested reader is referred to specialized discussions which may be found, for example, in the *American Handbook of Psychiatry* (New York: Basic Books, 1959).

Despite great diversity of symptomatology, the psychoneuroses have certain elements in common. For one thing, the patient is subjectively aware of some difficulty in living; he may be anxious; depressed; experience somatic difficulties (like gastrointestinal upsets, respiratory symptoms, headaches, and the like) for which physicians can find no organic basis; he may feel vaguely frustrated in his work and feel unable to achieve the vocational goals he has set himself; he may have difficulties in relating to other people in mutually satisfying ways (sexual problems are very common indicators of such difficulties, although they are now seen as a consequence or a concomitant of interpersonal problems rather

---

*The reference is to a group of conditions in which symptoms are essentially absent, but the person is irresponsible, emotionally shallow, and he may engage in antisocial behavior of various kinds without experiencing much anxiety or guilt.

than as their cause); or, he may simply feel vaguely unhappy with his lot.

Secondly, in order for a symptom picture to be seen as a manifestation of an intrapsychic conflict, exhaustive clinical study by a qualified professional person (psychiatrist, clinical psychologist) must demonstrate sufficient evidence of its existence. In other words, the person's life experiences and life pattern must give clues for inferring the presence of an unconscious conflict. Psychological tests are excellent techniques for this task, in conjunction with clinical interviews. For example, a person who has lost his life savings as a result of a currency devaluation and feels sad because he is facing old age without financial resources cannot be said to suffer from a neurotic conflict. Or, as Freud showed, we accept grief as a natural reaction to the loss of a loved one.* In short, in these instances external causes adequately "explain" the person's emotional state. On the other hand, we would hypothesize an unconscious conflict when a young attractive girl whose chances for marriage and a happy future seem excellent sees herself as ugly, repulsive, and unlovable, and is convinced that she is doomed to a life of unhappiness and lovelessness. Or, we would seriously consider that there is something amiss when a young man, having been jilted by his sweetheart, becomes despondent and deeply depressed for several years and makes repeated attempts to commit suicide. In these situations the emotional reaction is incommensurate with the circumstances, or cannot be accounted for on the basis of known factors. However, as already indicated, there usually must be present sufficient evidence in the person's past history to lend plausibility to the hypothesis of an unconscious conflict. Ignorance of antecedent causes is no justification in itself for assuming a neurotic conflict. On the other hand, neurotic conflicts are characterized by mental and/or physical symptoms which cannot be explained on the basis of the person's current life situation. That is, part of the conflict, as we have seen, is unconscious (as far as the patient is concerned). Stated otherwise, psychic forces, which are unacceptable to the person's conscious ego, seek and find expression through symptomatic behavior or feelings.

*In a widely quoted passage, Freud asserted that the most psychoanalysis can do is to transform neurotic misery into ordinary human unhappiness.

The Transference Relationship

Now the question may be raised: why not simply inform the person of the nature of his unconscious conflict and thereby relieve him of his suffering? The fact is that this procedure does not work. As Freud stated, its effectiveness is comparable to that of distributing printed menus to a hungry population. For a neurotic conflict to be resolved or ameliorated it is necessary to effect a dynamic change in the patient. Something about his feelings and attitudes which are part and parcel of his conflict must undergo modification in order for a therapeutic change to occur. The patient often does lack cognitive knowledge about the forces that motivate him, but, more than that, his *emotional reactions and attitudes* are faulty. Suppose a worker tends to get angry when given an order by his boss and through defiant behavior provokes the superior into punitive actions. Telling him that he is living out a conflict that he once had with his father in and of itself does not abolish the troublesome situation. Perhaps he knew it already, but in any case it makes little difference. What he has to learn is to adopt new (and more adaptive) techniques in relation to authority figures. In this process it may be helpful to him to gain an understanding of his defiance toward his father, the childhood reasons for this attitude, and the way his anachronistic behavior interferes with his current interpersonal relations. But this learning has to take place in a meaningful context, and as a result he must learn to feel and to behave differently. This meaningful context is provided by the *transference* relationship to the therapist. The therapeutic learning occurs as the patient begins to act out (relive) with the therapist the problem he had with his father. As the therapist succeeds in demonstrating to the patient that he is unwittingly reenacting with the therapist an important problems that once existed between the patient and his father, and as the patient comes to appreciate the emotional ramifications of his feelings and reactions, an intrapsychic change often occurs, and the patient comes to see the therapist (and other adults) more realistically rather than as personifications of the past.

Resolution of a Conflict

An intrapsychic conflict thus can be resolved to the extent that it can be *revived* in the therapeutic situation and become a conflict *in the present*. This is the reason for Freud's belief that only the transference neuroses are basically amenable to psycho-analytic therapy: the essence of psychoanalytic therapy consists of evoking new editions of old conflicts (called in orthodox psycho-analysis the *transference neurosis*) and providing an opportunity for their resolution along more adaptive (adult) lines. To the extent that the therapist succeeds in (1) making possible the emergence and development of transference feelings on the part of the patient and (2) demonstrating to him the anachronistic and self-defeating character of his transference manifestations—to that extent he is helping the patient to overcome his neurotic difficulties. In this task he relies on his own understanding of psychodynamics, tact, maturity, and empathy. He must also avoid emotional entangle-ments with the patient, which would make him a co-actor or collaborator in the very conflicts which he is helping the patient to resolve. He must remain neutral, and yet communicate an abiding friendly interest in the patient. Above all, he must facilitate in the patient the development of a sense of *trust* in the stability, relia-bility, and integrity of the therapist and the therapeutic relationship.

The Significance of Transference

The concept of the transference is of signal importance for psychoanalysis as a theory as well as a method of psychotherapy. In its significance and implications it is second to no other concept in Freud's system. Indeed, it is the fulcrum upon which psycho-analytic therapy— and all dynamic therapies based upon it—turns. For this reason it is necessary to gain a thorough understanding of this key concept.

A brief historical digression will aid in this task, and it will also demonstrate how Freud succeeded in turning what first ap-peared to be an insurmountable obstacle in therapy to a thera-peutic weapon of the first magnitude. His genius is shown nowhere more clearly than in this process.

As we have seen in Chapter 1, Freud began his collaboration with the older and highly respected Viennese physician, Josef Breuer, who had earlier evinced an interest in the treatment of hysteria. They observed that female patients (originally it was thought that hysteria occurred only in women) in the course of hypnotic treatment developed emotional attachments to their thera-pist, which at the time seemed to be a most unwelcome complica-tion. As far as Breuer knew, he did nothing to encourage this erotic interest which his women patients began to show toward him. It simply made no sense to Breuer that young women should suddenly fall in love with a middle-aged man who had done nothing to encourage such feelings, and who, realistically, considered himself a rather unsuitable object for their affection. Being thoroughly imbued with Victorian notions of sexuality, which were current in Vienna as elsewhere on the continent at the time, Breuer became quite alarmed at this unwelcome development. Not so Freud. Instead of shrinking back from these emotional attachments, Freud approached them as any other phenomenon in nature: he asked himself about their meaning in the context of the patient-therapist relationship. Eventually he concluded that, rather than being an obstacle to the treatment, the patient's emotional manifestations were an integral part of his very "illness." Freud came to see that the strong feelings which the patient was developing toward the therapist could not be explained on the basis of their *current* interaction. Nevertheless, as far as the patient was concerned, the feelings were as real as anything in the world. Freud came to the conclusion that the patient was *transferring* to the therapist feelings that he had at one time felt toward significant persons in his life—usually one or both of his parents—and while the circumstances of the patient's life had, of course, markedly changed since childhood, the feelings had not. In fact, Freud reasoned, it was this very tendency of his patients to experience toward present-day persons (*objects*) feeling that intrinsically had nothing to do with these persons that constituted the core of the patient's illness. It must be mentioned here that while at first the observations dealt primarily with erotic, positive feelings, Freud soon noted that when these feelings were not reciprocated by the therapist, they had an uncanny tendency to turn into the opposite. Thus, the therapist became the recipient of hostile, angry, hateful feelings, which, realistically, made as little sense as the earlier, positive ones. The patient, as Freud put it, thus wanted a cure through love. He also realized that it would be unethical to reciprocate the patient's feelings, and that in any case it would not help. The remarkable thing about all these happenings was that Freud managed to remain a dispassionate observer, who was as little impressed by, or responsive to, the patient's positive feelings as he was to the negative ones. Instead, he developed a technique for dealing with them. This technique, in its various forms, has come to be known as *interpretation,* and represents the major technical intervention in psychoanalysis and analytically oriented psychotherapy to this day.

The Role of Transference in Therapy

In its bare essence this technique consisted of efforts to demonstrate to the patient the anachronistic character of his feelings vis-á-vis the therapist and their inappropriateness in the patient's life as an adult. Thus, if the therapist remained essentially neutral and did nothing either to evoke or to suppress the patient's feelings, the latter eventually came to see that, while undisputedly real, they had no place in his life as an adult. This process was greatly facilitated, Freud discovered, when the therapist succeeded in linking the patient's feelings in the present to situations in his childhood which, consciously, the patient had long forgotten, but which on a feeling level had remained alive, albeit disguised and repressed. Occasionally, patients would remember specific incidents in their early lives, to which they could link their transference feelings, but sometimes even protracted efforts remained fruitless. When psycholanalysis first emerged as a method of treatment, Freud believed that the recall of repressed memories ("the lifting of the *infantile amnesia"*) was crucial for the patient's improvement. Therapy was considered nearing its termination when early memories were being recalled. However, clinical experience showed that often the infantile amnesia could not be lifted and the patient still improved, or the converse was true. The essential therapeutic factor evidently lay elsewhere. Indeed, as Freud came to realize, it was the totality of the therapist-relationship as it evolved over an extended period of time and the slow, painstaking process of *working through* which accounted for therapeutic change. In this process, the patient's transference distortions are being analyzed, which results in a strengthening of the patient's ego—the goal of any psychotherapy. Stated otherwise, as the patient gradually comes to trust the therapist and the therapeutic situation, he begins to reexperience conflicts which had been repressed since early childhood and which, as such, rarely ever were conscious. Thus, what frequently emerges are not specific memories but feelings and attitudes which become directed toward the therapist. Furthermore, what ultimately counts in therapy is the patient's *emotional experience* in therapy and the manner in which the therapist deals with it. There is nothing as convincing to the patient as what he experiences *on a feeling level* in relation to the therapist, which led Freud to observe that nothing that is experienced in the transference situation is ever forgotten,

The essence of psychoanalytic work consists of (1) the therapist's neutrality, awakening in the patient infantile feelings and reaction patterns which are "pushing upward" seeking expression; (2) the patient's reexperiencing them in the transference situation, (3) understanding them with the help of the therapist as repetitions or new editions of old conflicts, and (4) the therapist's placing them in historical perspective. Once this sequence has occurred, Freud found that the discovery of new and better solutions of these early conflicts could be safely left to the patient, and that he needed little help, if any, from the therapist in accomplishing this task. In other words, once an unconscious conflict has been transformed into a conscious one, the patient's adult ego is quite capable of solving it. Epigrammatically, Freud summed up the task of analytic therapy in the words: "Where id was, there shall ego be."

In theory, the foregoing sequence certainly sounds ingenious and elegant in its simplicity. In practice, the resolution of a transference neurosis is a stony road which is beset with many difficulties and which imposes rigorous demands and sacrifices on both patient and therapist. Freud clearly saw it as work, and the term "working through" was coined to describe the labors which the patient has to accomplish to resolve his neurotic difficulties. What is the nature of the obstacles and how can they be overcome?

The Therapist's Task

In order to understand the dynamics of transference, we have to take stock of the conflicting forces which are at work as well as their historical antecedents. First we must mention the "pact" into which the patient has entered with the therapist, as represented by the "basic rule." The patient has agreed to report his associations fully and without reserve. The therapist, for his part, has assured the patient of the utmost confidentiality and emotional neutrality. Soon the patient begins to collect evidence—through his interaction with the therapist—that the therapist means what he has promised. The patient is neither blamed nor punished, but neither is he applauded or praised. He receives neither signs of rejection nor proofs of love. If one's self-esteem is low—and no patient in psychotherapy is blessed with an excess of self-esteem—the absence of censure for anger, hostility, provocations, misdeeds (real or imagined), etc. is a great relief indeed. But in entering the "pact" with the therapist, the patient inevitably leaves out of account or grossly underestimates the extent and depth of his expectations from the therapist. Unconsciously, he sees in him an all-loving mother, an all-forgiving father, but he also projects onto him his sense of guilt, his need for punishment, and other excessive demands and ungratified wishes dating back to early childhood. Many of these expectations are utterly contradictory. For instance, the patient may complain of his dependence on the opinion of others, while at the same time meeting with intense anger and resentment the slightest suggestion from another person. He may wish for demonstrations of friendship, allegiance, loyalty, and love, and yet violently disparage the person who might make a friendly overture. Or, he is desperately afraid of punishment, yet he will continually rebel against the imposition of an external control, and so on.

Now it must be kept in mind (and the therapist is trained never to forget it) that the patient feels and acts the way he does not out of "badness" or orneriness, but because he cannot help it. He feels and acts the way he does toward others because he once was—and what is more important, *still is*—an intensely unhappy, disappointed and disillusioned person, who from early childhood on has tried unsuccessfully to get along with other people, and who, in most instances, has had inadequate help from his parents to master the all-important task of growing up emotionally. He has failed in learning techniques for appropriate, effective, and satisfying interactions with other people, but he also has been failed by the people on whom as a child he was dependent, and to whom he looked for guidance, love, and support. Yet, the parents too— and this is the tragedy of neurotic misery and of human existence— usually did not mistreat, pamper, abuse, or neglect the child out of maliciousness of evil intentions; they did the best they could within the limitations set by their own neurotic problems in living. Unhappily, the best was not good enough. And one must not forget either the exigencies and vicissitudes of life which play such an important role in neurotic disturbance: illness or premature death of a parent, poverty which requires a mother to work instead of caring for her children, a father's job which takes him away from his children on long business trips, and so forth.

So the therapist, from the first to the last hour of therapy, attempts to play the benevolent but neutral role of a mature adult. To be sure, this is an ideal which can never be fully realized, because the therapist is a human being, with his own past, developmental history, and emotional problems. But his training, and particularly his personal analysis, have equipped him to understand himself and the emotional problems of others. He has gained an appreciation of the common humanity in all persons and the problems to which they are prone. Thus, while not perfect, he often succeeds in mitigating, ameliorating, and at times fully resolving the conflicts in which the patient is embroiled. His own maturity constitutes the red thread of rationality and reasonableness which runs through therapy. Thus, the therapist comes to represent a model of reality for the patient which can and does serve him as an example. Ideally, this model represents the essential aspects of reality at its best and it provides the patient with a human relationship which is truly unique. From this base of operations the therapist does his work. He can stay largely uninvolved emotionally because his demands upon the patient are strictly circumscribed. He expects to get paid for his labors; he expects the patient to keep his appointed hours; he expects him to comply with the "basic rule"; and he expects the patient to respect the therapist's rights of privacy and property. But beyond these limitations, the patient enjoys the largest possible freedom to feel and to experience the gamut of human emotions. He can be hostile and aggressive without fearing retaliation; he can express positive feelings of affection and love without fearing that he is either rejected or exploited; he need never be concerned about the therapist's personal feelings; in short, he can be himself in therapy as he can be himself nowhere else. The therapist bends his energies upon understanding the patient and his feelings. He accomplishes this often difficult feat through *empathy,* the ability to resonate to the emotional experience of others. Often he can anticipate what the patient is about to feel but more often he observes and participates empathically, while at the same time remaining emotionally uninvolved. In one psychoanalyst's meaningful phrase: he LISTENS.

The therapist's reliability and trustworthiness, of course, must be experienced by the patient in order to be accepted as reality. Hopefully, as the therapeutic relationship continues, the patient has ample opportunity to test the stability of the relationship. And, this is exactly what the patient—every patient—does. He (unconsciously) attempts to cajole, manipulate, provoke, seduce, coerce, and he uses all the maneuvers that are open to a child to deal with an adult who does not do his bidding. If the therapist proves equal to these stratagems, if he succeeds in identifying them for what they are—namely desperate attempts to control his own feelings through controlling a significant adult—he performs an important therapeutic function. The patient can then come to see the therapist for what he is and always has been: a mature adult in present-day reality, whose job it is to help the patient. To be sure, no one will begrudge the therapist a sense of satisfaction when ultimately he sees his labors rewarded by the patient's improvement through growing up emotionally. This is an intangible reward, which the therapist shares with any good parent who sees his child develop into an independent, self-reliant, and strong adult.

Transference in Action

We see, then, that throughout therapy the patient's *real* relationship with the therapist, as opposed to his unconscious expectations, provides a "corrective emotional experience" which the patient needs. It also permits the patient to do the hard work which is expected of him, and it provides him with a genuine helper for whom he may retain a life-long affection and gratitude. Therapy, in a sense, is a continual interplay between the forces of present-day reality and the forces of childhood which continually pull back the patient to earlier, immature modes of relatedness. And it is the therapist's job to help the patient sort out emotionally what is *real* and what is *transferred*.

The techniques which the patient unwittingly employs with a tenacity which is difficult to express in words are the defenses which he originally developed as a child to deal with his own violent and powerful impulses, the difficulties he had in relating to his parents who were unable to serve as adequate models of adult reality, and unfortunate life experiences over which the patient, as well as his parents, were unable to exercise control.

This battle reaches the depth and intensity which it does because the feelings against which the patient is defending himself are without exception exceedingly *painful* ones. This also explains why transference becomes the most powerful resistance in therapy.

Behind the stubborn defenses always hides a child who feels utterly
unhappy, helpless, abandoned, disgruntled, and profoundly disillusioned. The reliving of these painful experiences is the essence
of psychotherapy. It is a task which cannot be spared the patient,
and it is the price which the patient has to pay for "getting well,"
and growing up. For this reason, the therapist, in addition to his
technical skill and personality attributes which have already been
mentioned, must have tact, compassion, patience, and tolerance.
Although therapy is always a painful experience, it becomes bear-
able for the patient because he has on his side the emotional support, the unswerving interest, and the enduring good will of the
therapist.

Stated otherwise, the therapist aids the patient's ego to face
the conflicts and the unhappiness to which it once fell victim because of its weakness and immaturity. The therapist, allying himself
with the patient's mature ego, persuades it, as it were, to face once
more the painful feelings from which it once shrank back. The
difference is that (1) the patient's ego is not really as weak and
vulnerable as it once was since the patient is no longer a helpless
child, and (2) it now has a powerful ally in the person of the
therapist who helps to brave the storm. The therapist thus holds
out the promise that while the feelings that lie hidden in the patient
are the same as they ever were, there is no longer the need to deal
with them by means of the old techniques (chiefly repression)
which the patient could not help employing when he was a small
child.

The crucial importance of transference in psychotherapy is
best summarized in Freud's own words:

> The theory of repression is the corner-stone on which
> the whole structure of psycho-analysis rests. It is the most
> essential part of it; and yet it is nothing but a theoretical
> formulation of a phenomenon which may be observed as often
> as one pleases if one undertakes an analysis of a neurotic
> without resorting to hypnosis. In such cases one comes across
> a resistance which opposes the work of analysis and in order
> to frustrate it pleads a failure of memory. The use of hypnosis
> was bound to hide this resistance; the history of psycho-
> analysis proper, therefore, only begins with the new technique
> that dispenses with hypnosis. The theoretical consideration of
> the fact that this resistance coincides with an amnesia leads

inevitably to the view of unconscious mental actitvity which is peculiar to psycho-analysis and which, too, distinguishes it quite clearly from philosophical speculations about the unconscious. It may thus be said that the theory of psychoanalysis is an attempt to account for two striking and unexpected facts of observation which emerge whenever an attempt is made to trace the symptoms of a neurotic back to their sources in his past life: the facts of transference and resistance. *Any line of investigation which recognizes these two facts and takes them as the starting-point of its work has a right to call itself psycho-analysis,* even though it arrives at results other than my own. But anyone who takes up other sides of the problem while avoiding these two hypotheses will hardly escape a charge of misappropriation of property by attempted impersonation, if he persists in calling himself a psycho-analyst.

("On the History of the Psychoanalytic Movement,"
Standard Edition, 14, p. 16;
emphasis supplied.)

CHAPTER **8**

The Problem of
Therapeutic Change

In the last chapter we learned something about the manner in which psychoanalysis as a method of treatment attempts to bring about therapeutic changes in the patient's personality. In this endeavor the main focus rests on the revival of childhood conflicts in the patient's relationship to the therapist and the resolution of these conflicts by means of interpretations offered at appropriate times by the therapist. In other words, psychoanalysis as a method of therapy is characterized by its emphasis on *transference phenomena*. It has also become apparent throughout this volume that there is a close parallel between psychoanalysis as a theory dealing with the development of the personality, and psychoanalysis as a method of treatment. This close relationship is largely a function of the manner in which psychoanalysis evolved. Initially, Freud was primarily interested in developing a method of treatment, and his theory of personality development emerged from reconstructions of the patient's past made during the course of therapy. The aim of psychoanalytic psychotherapy, in essence, is to provide the patient with an "after-education" (Freud's term), or, to put it somewhat differently, to effect corrections in the patient's personality structure, which under more favorable circumstances would have occurred in the natural process of growing up.

How does psychoanalysis as a method of treatment differ from other methods of psychotherapy? Clearly, many people seek the services of a psychotherapist for various problems in living, and only a very small percentage of patients undergo psychoanalysis in the "orthodox" Freudian sense. Are the personality changes achieved by other methods less impressive, less lasting, or altogether different?

Answers to these questions are difficult to give and would involve technical discussions which lie beyond the scope of this treatise. Furthermore, we would be entering a highly controversial field, which is beset by disputes among representatives of rival "schools" of psychotherapy. Nevertheless, an attempt at clarification is in order, although it should be pointed out that just as different theoretical orientations in psychotherapy (e.g., the theories of Carl Gustav Jung, Alfred Adler, Harry Stack Sullivan, Carl Rogers, existentialism, learning theory — to name but a few) diverge in their conceptualizations of the problems, so they differ in their goals and the kinds of changes their respective adherents purport to achieve. Conclusive research is still a thing of the future —indeed, controlled investigations designed to answer these and other thorny questions were not begun until about 1940—a rather short time span in the history of any science.

Problems of Research

The measurement of personality and personality change is intimately tied to these questions, and such measurements are by no means as precise as researchers would like them to be. Furthermore, it is exceedingly difficult to isolate the hypothesized therapeutic factors to which changes in the person's total functioning are attributed. A moment's reflection will show that people change throughout their lives—they change jobs, get married or divorced, undergo biological changes as a result of aging, suffer losses due to illness or bereavement, or they get "lucky breaks," all of which may influence their emotional difficulties and conflicts for better or for worse. Since we cannot place people in cages like laboratory animals during the course of psychotherapy and thus control life experiences outside of therapy, we are seriously handicapped in studying the effects of a particular method of psychotherapy, including psychoanalysis. There always remains the gnawing question: are the changes which occurred during and following therapy a function of the particular method; are they due to the personal attributes of the therapist; or would they have occurred without professional intervention? In short, the task of comparing the *relative efficacy* of different forms of psychotherapy, because of the foregoing and other technical difficulties, largely lies beyond the capabilities of contemporary research.

In the light of these obstacles some critics have drawn the unwarranted conclusion that psychotherapy has failed to demonstrate convincingly its effectiveness, and that consequently (a clear *non sequitur*) it is of questionable value. This criticism has been directed with particular vehemence against psychoanalysis as the most ambitious but also the most costly, time-consuming, and arduous form of psychotherapy. It should be apparent that failure to demonstrate the efficacy of a treatment technique in terms which are acceptable to the "hard-nosed" critic is not tantamount to a proof of its ineffectiveness. The only statement which can be made at the present state of knowledge is that (a) clinical experience (observations by psychotherapists and their patients) abundantly supports the belief that beneficial results do result from psychotherapy in an appreciable percentage of the patients treated, and that these changes often are quite dramatic; (b) the superiority of one method of psychotherapy over any other form is an unsettled issue; and (c) neither psychoanalysis nor any other form of psychotherapy offers a panacea for *all* of man's emotional ills and difficulties in living. Most treatment techniques in the field of medicine can claim no more. Or, if one prefers the model of education (which may be more appropriate): There are many ways in which learning can occur, of which the technique employed by a particular teacher is only one. Similarly, in psychotherapy desirable personality changes can occur in a variety of ways. The theoretical framework to which the therapist subscribes and the technical operations he employs may be only one contributing factor. Indeed, there are suggestions that psychotherapeutic changes are rather similar, irrespective of the therapist's "school." If this be true, it would be a matter of personal preference *how* one wishes to conceptualize these changes. Since we have been dealing with Freudian theory, we have been discussing psychotherapy in terms of psychoanalytic concepts. Someone else may wish to employ different terms, and in fact many theorists and therapists have done so. As the field develops, many differences between schools may prove to be more apparent than real, which is not to assert that there may not be unique factors in a particular system. The systematic utilization of the transference as the fulcrum of therapeutic change in psychoanalysis may be one such factor.

Overemphasis on the Past?

Psychoanalysis, as we have seen, searches for the origins of the patient's current difficulties in his early life experience, particularly traumas he sustained in the earliest years of his life when his ego was weak and he was highly impressionable. Because of his immaturity, the strength of his instinctual strivings, constitutional and hereditary factors (which are as yet poorly understood), and unhappy experiences with parental figures, the person's ego had to resort to emergency measures to cope with these vicissitudes. These emergency measures are the defenses (notably repression), which often restrict the ego's free functioning and produce inhibitions and neurotic symptoms. Psychoanalysis attempts to deal with these problems by attempting to revive the early threatening situations in the transference, and to give them a different outcome. In other words, the patient is forced to reexperience his early conflicts in psychoanalysis, but the new relationship to the therapist (which is significantly different from the parent-child relationship) holds out the hope that the childhood conflict, when revived and reexperienced in a safer situation, can be resolved in more adaptive ways than was possible when the patient was in fact an immature, helpless child.

Psychoanalysis is often acccused of an undue preoccupation with the patient's past, especially his early childhood, allegedly at the expense of his difficulties in the present. This criticism is largely unfounded. Psychoanalysis deals with the past only insofar as it still influences the patient's personality functioning as an adult. The fact that the patient produces transference manifestations in the therapeutic relationship is seen as the strongest evidence that problems of the past are still "alive" and troublesome in the present. Psychoanalysis cannot reactivate conflicts that were once successfully resolved and to which the patient has found viable and adaptive solutions. It does attempt to deal with emotional conflicts that are still active in the present, in the sense of causing the patient emotional suffering and producing unwanted (ego-alien) neurotic symptoms. In the treatment itself, there is a continual weaving back and forth between present and past, and the therapist attempts to demonstrate to the patient that his conflicts and symptoms are meaningful in the context of his early life experience. The emphasis rests on the *feelings and emotions that are experienced by the patient in the present, particularly in relation to the therapist.*

Psychoanalysis and Other Forms of Therapy

Psychoanalytic therapy attempts to abolish the original conflict by demonstrating to the patient its irrational and anachronistic character. Therapy, Freud believed, can do little about modifying the patient's instinctual strivings, but it can do a great deal to help the patient's ego handle them in different (more adaptive, more adult) ways. The ego, in short, gains a new mastery over instinctual impulses and strivings, and thus grows in flexibility, reasonableness, and competence. No longer is the patient driven compulsively by unconscious forces he does not understand, but he becomes to a great extent a "master in his own house," and he does things because *he wants* to, not because something within him forces him.

Thus, psychoanalysis (at least in theory) is a radical treatment in that its objective is to *abolish* conflicts both within the person and in his relations with others, and it accomplishes this goal through a restructuration of the mental apparatus, notably a strengthening of the patient's ego.

Other forms of psychotherapy may have different objectives. For example, it may be possible, in the case of relatively minor disturbances, to strengthen the patient's defenses without dealing with the repressed forces. Instead of reviving the psychic conflict in the transference and dealing with the underlying impulses, it may be more efficient in many instances to come directly to the aid of the patient's beleaguered ego. Such forms of therapy leave essentially untouched the patient's relationship to the therapist (the transference), but largely use it for the purpose of supporting the patient's ego in its struggles against impulses which are experienced as unwelcome intruders. For example, the therapist's attempt to induce the patient to expose himself to a subjectively threatening situation (e.g., a phobia), by telling him authoritatively that the feared consequences will not ensue, represents an instance of this sort. Here the therapist uses his authority to strengthen the patient's ego through direct suggestions. A crucial factor in the relative promise of various treatments is the strength of the patient's ego and its maturity as demonstrated by previous successes in adaptation.

It seems inappropriate to draw rigid lines between "supportive" therapy and "psychoanalysis" because—at least in this writer's opinion—techniques shade into each other, and all therapists, in practice, seem to use a combination of techniques. Other authors notwithstanding—a number of whom make sharp distinctions between "psychoanalysis" and "psychotherapy"—it appears that the differences are of degree, not of kind. It is undeniable, however, that psychoanalysis in its purest form places maximum emphasis on the transference and the interpretation of transference phenomena. The psychotherapist (in contradistinction to the psychoanalyst) uses a wider variety of techniques, and employs his personal influences in a broader and less "controlled" sense. He is less averse to making suggestions, giving recommendations, and even direct advice. Most forms of psychotherapy (e.g., counseling, so-called brief psychotherapy, "crisis-intervention," etc.) are clearly of the latter variety. Psychoanalysis, in contrast, employs a more indirect approach, encourages the patient to find his own solutions, and avoids suggestion and advice. To reiterate, its aim is to effect a change in the dynamic balance of the psychic apparatus and it is concerned with the psychic forces and their alignment. From this inner alignment beneficial changes in the person's transactions with the outside world are seen to flow.

It is as yet a moot question which approach is better. In some ways, this is analogous to asking whether an appendectomy or a tonsillectomy is "better." The answer depends on the nature and severity of the problem, the patient's psychological status, his level of maturity, his motivation to work toward a cure and his ability and willingness to invest time, money, and energy in intensive and prolonged psychotherapy. Unfortunately, it has been documented* that the form of therapy a patient receives often bears a greater relationship to his financial status than to other factors; however, it is time to bury the notion that, in comparison with psychoanalysis, all other forms of psychotherapy are "second-class" or inferior. Most analysts would agree with this statement, although it lingers in the minds of many patients. The number of patients who are either suited for or financially able to afford

*Hollingshead, A. B., & Redlich, F. C., *Social Class and Mental Illness*, (New York, Wiley, 1958).

psychoanalysis in the strict sense is minute compared to the large number of people who can and do benefit from other forms of psychotherapy.

On the other hand, it must be admitted that psychoanalysts have maintained that intensive psychoanalysis produces a unique restructuring of the total personality, which is supposedly unobtainable by other forms of psychotherapy or as a result of life experiences. While this may be true, conclusive evidence is lacking.

The search for shorter, more efficient, and less expensive methods of psychotherapy has been a persistent one, and was recognized by Freud himself. Great impetus for this objective has been given by the latter-day interest in problems of mental health and illness, as epitomized by the report of a commission appointed by the Congress of the United States.* Certainly, it cannot be asserted that there is a one-to-one relationship between length, intensity, and cost of therapy on the one hand and favorableness of outcome on the other. In recent years, a number of treatment methods have come to the fore, many of which have sharply taken issue with the theory and practice of psychoanalysis. The need for more efficient, less expensive, and less demanding forms of psychotherapy is undeniably real, and with the increasing shortages in professional manpower arising from the population explosion, the magnitude of the problem will become more severe during the next decades. In this connection, too, we must mention the phenomenal impact of the so-called psychoactive drugs, which, beginning in the 1950's, have flooded the market, promising relief from tensions, anxiety, and various psychic disturbances. As far as the evidence goes, these drugs often provide relief but they don't cure. Broadly speaking, the public has become much more keenly aware of emotional problems, their origins, consequences, and treatment.

Education vs. Cure

To reiterate a point which has been made throughout this volume: Psychic conflicts are partly a function of the person's life experience; partly they are a function of his constitution and heredity; and partly they are a function of the process of biological

*Joint Commission on Mental Illness and Health. *Action for Mental Health.* (New York, Basic Books, 1961).

and psychological development in a particular culture which imposes restrictions on the free and untrammeled expression of the individual's native tendencies. Insofar as psychic conflicts are "learned"—and there is good evidence to show that many are— they can be unlearned and more efficient techniques of getting along with oneself and others can be substituted. Freud showed that such re-learning can take place and he evolved an ingenious technique for accomplishing this end. He never had any illusions that early patterns of feeling and behaving are deeply entrenched and difficult to modify. Learning always takes time; and emotional learning, in particular, is extraordinarily tedious and hard. Perhaps this learning can be facilitated and accelerated by as yet undreamed-of techniques. In this process, pharmacological agents may play an important part and enhance the patient's motivation for change. Psychotherapy, unlike other forms of learning, must include the *unlearning* of previously acquired faulty techniques, in addition to learning new, more adaptive ones. Psychotherapy, like education, may be steadily improved, streamlined, and accelerated. Yet, just as any educational process encounters limits set by the student's native endowment, motivation, previous life experience, and various socio-environmental factors, the same is true of psychotherapy. So far, no one has lost faith in education because it is less than perfect. No more, but also no less, should be expected of the different forms of psychotherapy.

At this point the perceptive reader may ask: At various times neurosis has been described as a disorder analogous to a disease, but now psychotherapy is said to be a learning process. Is psychotherapy then a form of medical treatment or is it education? The question is certainly justified, and this much is clear: Psychotherapy is very different from any form of medical treatment in which the patient plays a passive role and is ministered to by his physician. If one is ill with a virus infection it makes very little difference what his attitude about the virus happens to be, or for that matter how one views an injection of penicillin. As we have seen, psychotherapy proceeds on the basis of very different assumptions, and the word "patient" is at best ambiguous. By the same token, the therapist's role is not that of a physician in the ordinary sense. The relationship between the two participants comes closer to that between master and student, although the fit is not perfect, either.

Freud's position on the subject was clear and explicit. While his own training had been in medicine, he never considered himself a physician, and he felt very strongly that psychoanalysis was not a medical specialty. He regarded himself as a psychologist, and he hoped that psychoanalysis would become a part of general psychology. He felt particularly strongly that medical training was detrimental to the proper attitude of the psychotherapist:

> A knowledge of the anatomy of the metatarsal bones, of the properties of carbohydrates, of the courses of the cranial nerves, of all that medicine has discovered as to bacillary infection and means to prevent it, or of serum reactions, or neoplasms—all this is of the greatest value in itself but will take him [the analyst] nowhere. It will not directly help him to understand and cure a neurosis, nor does this sort of knowledge sharpen the intellectual faculties on which his professional activities will make such demands. The analyst's experience lies in another world from that of pathology, with other phenomena and other laws. However philosophy may bridge the gap between physical and mental, it still exists for practical purposes, and our practice on each side of it must differ accordingly.
>
> *The Question of Lay Analysis,* p. 119.

Freud's views to the contrary, psychoanalysis—particularly in the United States—has become largely a medical specialty, which accounts for the fact that the majority of analysts in this country have earned the M.D. degree and completed a residency in psychiatry before they entered psychoanalytic training. The fact, however, remains that all psychotherapists, irrespective of their background training, employ psychological techniques which in turn are based on psychological principles. Future research, therefore, must look to psychology for answers to the unresolved problems surrounding the functions of the human mind. While no one can foretell the future, it seems reasonable to assume that as psychology succeeds in advancing our understanding of the principles of learning it will also provide better answers on how to change a person's feelings, attitudes, and actions.

CHAPTER **9**

Concluding Comments

In the preceding chapters, we have attempted to give a brief overview of the salient features of psychoanalytic theory, stressing the linkage between the basic clinical observations and the theoretical formulations by means of which Freud tried to systematize them. Of necessity, it has not been possible to go into numerous theoretical intricacies, nor can a claim for completeness be advanced in other respects. The interested reader is referred to more comprehensive and exhaustive presentations, of which there are many (see selected references). In the closing pages we shall make brief reference to the pervasive influence of Freud's discoveries on human affairs in the twentieth century.

In the early years Freud's writings were largely ignored, and his *magnum opus, The Interpretation of Dreams* (1900) sold only a few hundred copies at the time. However, Freud had already made the unhappy discovery that "Psychoanalysis brings out the worst in everyone" (*Standard Edition,* 14, p. 39). The medical profession in Vienna had turned its back on Freud as soon as he began to stress sexual factors in the etiology of hysteria, forcing him into professional isolation which lasted many years. With the publication of his later writings his influence increased, but so did the vituperative attacks from many quarters, which often took crass form. At a Congress of German Neurologists and Psychiatrists in 1910, when Freud's theories were mentioned, one professor shouted: "This is not a topic for discussion at a scientific meeting; it is a matter for the police!" Freud never entered these polemics, taking the position that in any field of scientific endeavor nothing is ever settled by argument. Understandably, however, he could not refrain from becoming embittered by the vicious attacks and vilifications which descended upon his head not only from physicians and psychiatrists, but from members of other professions, many of whom had only the scantest familiarity with his views and their empirical bases. Superficial acquaintance with Freudian psychology and resulting misunderstandings indeed persist to this day. Sober and objective discussion of the issues is still the exception rather than the rule.

Partly as a reaction to these unsavory manifestations of the *Zeitgeist,* psychoanalysts were forced outside the academic community and compelled to set up their own institutes and organizations. This trend has continued to this day although, in the United States, psychoanalytic theory is taught in university departments (e.g., psychology, psychiatry). Still, training in the technique of psychoanalysis remains largely confined to separate institutes.

Since Freud's death in 1939 numerous developments have occurred within psychoanalytic theory, which have led to somewhat different emphases and more thorough exploration of some of its components. These newer trends and modifications cannot be dealt with in this book, and again the reader must be referred to more specialized treatises. It suffices to point out that the pillars of the theory which has been sketched in this essay have stood the test of time remarkably well. Indeed, clinical experience has abundantly corroborated Freud's basic observations and formulations. Like any scientific theory, Freudian theory is in a constant state of flux, and as time goes on we may expect to see further changes, additions, and reformulations.

It is interesting to note that Freud's influence in the United States, particularly since the end of the Second World War, has been incomparably greater than in Europe. Partly this is a function of the emigration of the most productive workers in the field of psychoanalysis and the antagonism toward psychoanalysis by the Nazis as well as by the Communist countries; partly it is a result of American receptiveness to Freud's teachings.

Freudian concepts have greatly influenced American psychiatry during the last decades, and even when Freud's contributions are not explicitly acknowledged, "dynamic" formulations of mental functioning and abnormality are unthinkable without Freud's work.

While academic psychology in the United States was slow to recognize and to accept psychoanalytic thinking, this picture has radically changed during the last two decades, notably with the rapid rise of clinical psychology as one of the major mental health professions. The situation has been similar in psychiatric social work, which benefited greatly from the teachings of Otto Rank, one of Freud's closest associates who came to the United States in the 1930's. There are today in New York City more psychoanalysts than in all countries of the world combined. All of these developments have culminated in a vigorous interest on the part of the public as well as the federal and state governments in problems of mental health and illness.

The social sciences, literature, painting, sculpture and many other fields have come to recognize and assimilate Freud's emphasis on unconscious factors in mental functioning. As the British anthropologist, Geoffrey Gorer,* aptly put it:

> Chiefly by diluted influence, Freud has profoundly modified our (and particularly American) attitudes toward children, child-rearing, and education, to the sick, the criminal, the insane. Because Freud lived and worked, the weak and the unhappy are often treated with a gentleness and charity and attempts at understanding which constitute one of the few changes in the climate of opinion in this century of which one need not be ashamed.

Freud correctly anticipated that psychoanalysis, as a method treatment, would have to be adapted to reach larger segments of the population, to whom the "classical" method would remain unavailable because of cost and other factors. Today there already are in existence numerous forms of psychotherapy which begin to approach this prediction. While psychoanalysis offers no miraculous solutions to human suffering and unhappiness any more than other remedies available to man, it provides a beacon for continued efforts to mitigate the destructive effects of unconscious factors in human relations through rational and humane means.

*Gorer, G. Freud's Influence. *The Encounter,* November 1958 (quoted by R. Waelder).

Suggestions for Further Reading

This list of annotated references has been compiled to provide the reader with authoritative sources, most of which are easily accessible. Included also are a number of books giving fuller accounts of the psychoanalytic theory. A number of the cited references contain comprehensive bibliographies which the reader may wish to consult for special topics. *The Standard Edition* will eventually include all of Freud's writings. A number of his works, judged most valuable for the beginning student, are listed separately. In addition to the *Standard Edition,* the five volumes of *Collected Papers* represents a valuable source. Many of Freud's major contributions are also available in paperback form. The authoritative translations by James Strachey are to be preferred in all instances.

Abraham, K. *Selected Papers on Psychoanalysis*. New York: Basic Books, 1953. A collection of important papers by one of Freud's outstanding students; technical.

Alexander, F., Eisenstein, & Grotjahn, M. (Eds.) *Psychoanalytic Pioneers*. New York: Basic Books, 1966. Biographical portraits of eminent collaborators and students of Freud, who played key roles in the development of psychoanalysis.

Fenichel, O. *The Psychoanalytical Theory of Neurosis*. New York: Norton, 1945. The most authoritative and systematic presentation of psychoanalytic theory from the clinical standpoint; requires serious study; extensive bibliography. Not recommended for the beginner.

Fine, R. *Freud: A Critical Re-Evaluation of His Theories*. New York: David McKay Co., 1962. A recent reassessment of Freudian theory; clear and readable.

Freud, Anna. *The Ego and the Mechanisms of Defense*. New York: International Universities Press, 1946. An important original contribution by Freud's daughter; represents an expansion of Freud's thinking.

Freud, S. *The Standard Edition of the Complete Psychological Works of Sigmund Freud*. (24 volumes) Under the general editorship of James Strachey. London: The Hogarth Press and the Institute of Psycho-Analysis, 1955- . The most recent English edition of Freud's works, superseding all previous translations and editions; still in progress of publication. Apart from the excellence of the translations, editorial notes and comments are extremely informative.

Of particular interest are the following writings, listed in order of appearance (dates refer to the first publication):

(with J. Breuer) *Studies on Hysteria* (1895).
The Interpretation of Dreams (1900).
The Psychopathology of Everyday Life (1901).
Jokes and their Relation to the Unconscious (1905).
Three Essays on the Theory of Sexuality (1905).
Totem and Taboo (1912-1913).
Introductory Lectures on Psychoanalysis. (A General Introduction to Psychoanalysis.) (1916-1917).
The Ego and the Id (1923).
Inhibitions, Symptoms and Anxiety. (The Problem of Anxiety) (1926).
The Question of Lay Analysis (1926).
Civilization and its Discontents (1930).
New Introductory Lectures on Psycho-Analysis (1938).
An Outline of Psycho-Analysis (1938).
Freud, S. *Collected Papers* (5 volumes). Translated by Alix and James Strachey. London: The Hogarth Press and the Institute of Psycho-Analysis, 1950. An earlier edition of selected writings; contains many of Freud's key contributions.
Fromm, E. *Man for Himself: An Inquiry into the Psychology of Ethics.* New York: Rinehart, 1947. A highly readable and stimulating work by one of the Neo-Freudians.
Glover, E. *The Technique of Psychoanalysis.* New York: International Universities Press, 1955. A first-rate exposition of analytic technique; technical.
Greenson, R. R. *The Technique and Practice of Psychoanalysis.* Volume I. New York: International Universities Press, 1967. A comprehensive technical exposition of psychoanalytic technique.
Hendrick, I. *Facts and Theories of Psychoanalysis* (3rd rev. ed.) New York: Knopf, 1958. An important secondary source, presents a clear exposition of analytic theory and practice.

Horney, Karen. *New Ways in Psychoanalysis.* New York: Norton, 1939. A readable treatise by an analyst who takes issue with some of Freud's basic conceptions and stresses cultural factors in the etiology of neurotic disturbances.

Jones, E. *The Life and Work of Sigmund Freud* (3 volumes). New York: Basic Books, 1953-1957. The standard biography on Freud by one of Freud's most ardent admirers and faithful associates. Outstanding both as a biographical study and as a description of the evolution of Freud's thought. A one-volume condensation is also available.

Kubie, L. S. *Practical and Theoretical Aspects of Psychoanalysis.* New York: International Universities Press, 1950. Another highly readable secondary source.

Menninger, K. *Theory of Psychoanalytic Technique.* New York: Basic Books, 1958. A recent exposition of the theory of psychoanalytic therapy; technical.

Munroe, Ruth L. *Schools of Psychoanalytic Thought.* New York: Dryden, 1955. A noteworthy comparative study of Freud's thought and the contributions of the major dissidents; intended for serious students; extensive bibliography.

Mullahy, P. *Oedipus: Myth and Complex.* New York: Grove Press, 1955. Written by a follower of Sullivan and influenced by the latter's thinking, critically compares Freudian theory to those of his major disciples.

Oberndorf, C. P. *A History of Psychoanalysis in America.* New York: Grune & Stratton, 1953. A historical account of psychoanalysis in the United States.

Pumpian-Mindlin, E. (Ed.) *Psychoanalysis as Science.* New York: Basic Books, 1952. A collection of critical papers dealing with the scientific status of psychoanalytic theory.

Rapaport, D. "The Structure of Psychoanalytic Theory: A Systematizing Attempt." *Psychol. Issues,* 2, No. 2 (Monograph #6). New York: International Universities Press, 1960. An excellent exposition of psychoanalytic theory by one of the foremost contemporary interpreters of psychoanalytic theory; technical.

Robert, Marthe. *The Psychoanalytic Revolution: Sigmund Freud's Life and Achievement.* New York: Harcourt, Brace, and World, 1966. A biography and appraisal.

Shakow, D. & Rapaport, D. "The Influence of Freud on American Psychology." *Psychol. Issues,* 4, No. 1. (Monograph #13).

New York: International Universities Press, 1964. A scholarly account of Freud's influence on American academic psychology.

Sullivan, H. S. *The Collected Works of Harry Stack Sullivan* (2 volumes). New York: Basic Books, 1964. A recently issued collection of papers by an American psychiatrist who was influenced by Freud but developed a theoretical system of his own.

Thompson, Clara. *Psychoanalysis: Evolution and Development.* New York: Hermitage House, 1950. A critical work by a co-worker of Sullivan's who questions some of Freud's basic assumptions, particularly his biological orientation; very readable.

Waelder, R. *Basic Theory of Psychoanalysis.* New York: International Universities Press, 1960. Another general exposition of psychoanalytic theory; readable but authoritative.

Whyte, L. L. *The Unconscious Before Freud.* New York: Basic Books, 1960. A historical study tracing the evolution of Freud's concept of the unconscious; specialized.

Zilboorg, G. & Henry, G. W. *A History of Medical Psychology.* New York: Norton, 1941. For those interested in the broader sweep of history.

GLOSSARY

In preparing this Glossary, the following sources have been consulted:
Hendrick, I. *Facts and Theories of psychoanalysis* (3rd Ed.). New York:
Alfred A. Knopf, 1958.
Hinsie, L. E. & Campbell, R. J. *Psychiatric Dictionary.* (3rd Ed.). New
York: Oxford University Press, 1960.
The assistance of Mr. Stuart Strenger is gratefully acknowledged.

abreaction. Discharge of emotion resulting from the recall of a repressed idea or memory; often used synonymously with *catharsis.*

affect. The subjective aspect of emotion; feeling.

aggression. One of the primary instincts; signifies action carried out
in a forceful way. Essentially destructive but when sublimated may
serve constructive ends.

anal period. The second major period of psychosexual development,
characterized by pleasurable sensations resulting from retention
or expulsion of bowel contents.

analysand. A person undergoing psychoanalysis.

analysis. See *psychoanalysis.*

anti-cathexis. Psychic energy associated with a given impulse which
is shifted to an impulse of an opposite character.

anxiety. An experience of dread accompanied by physiological symptoms such as disturbed breathing, increased heart rate, muscle tension, increased sweating, etc.

anxiety-hysteria. A psychoneurosis frequently characterized by phobias.

castration anxiety. Fear of loss or injury to the penis as fantasied
punishment for the gratification of incestuous desires. The term
is often used in a broad sense to denote inhibitions in assuming the
masculine role.

catharsis. See *abreaction.*

cathexis. Concentration of psychic energy upon an external or internal
object.

character. A person's enduring patterns of behavior, especially social
behavior.

censor. The influences which disguise the latent content (actual meaning) of the dream.

clinical psychology. That branch of psychology which focuses primarily upon the study, diagnosis, and treatment of psychological
disorders.

complex. A group of interrelated, emotionally-charged ideas which impel the individual to think, feel, and act in a habitual pattern. The important elements are unconscious.

compulsion. Action resulting from the need to perform an act or ritual despite the realization that it is irrational or purposeless.

condensation. See *dream*. The coincident representation of several unconscious wishes or objects by a single dream-image.

conflict. The opposition of intrapsychic impulses. The core of a conflict is typically unconscious.

conscience. See *superego*.

conscious (noun). That part of the mind of which the individual is or can become aware.

conversion symptom. See *hysteria*.

death instinct. An instinct whose derivatives (see *derivative*) consist of impulses to injure or destroy oneself or others, and whose ultimate aim is death.

defense mechanism. Any of a variety of unconscious reactions, usually involving repression, designed to protect the ego from the experience of anxiety or guilt associated with an unconscious wish or idea.

delay. Postponement of the gratification of an impulse because of the demands of the external world.

delusion. A false belief engendered without appropriate external stimulation and maintained despite incontrovertible evidence to the contrary.

derivative (noun). The energy of a repressed impulse which is displaced to an associatively-related but less dangerous impulse.

determinism. The scientific view that all events (including human thoughts, feelings, and actions) are caused.

displacement. The shifting of psychic energy from one object to another. The phenomenon commonly occurs in waking life as well as in dreams. *E.g.,* a man who experiences anger toward a superior but, being afraid of the consequences, vents the feelings upon his wife.

dream work. The process by which a dream is evolved through the mechanisms of condensation, displacement, and symbolization.

drive. See *instinct*.

dynamics. See *psychodynamics*.

ego. That part of the personality which mediates between the person and reality. It develops defenses against id and superego impulses and controls cognition, perception, and volition. The ego is governed by the reality-principle.

ego-alien. See *ego-syntonic*.

egocentricity. Self-centeredness; viewing everything in relation to one's own self-interest.

ego ideal. An image of what one aspires to be, developing out of identifications with others; part of the superego.

ego psychology. That trend in psychoanalysis which emphasizes the ego functions of the personality in theory, research, and clinical practice.

ego-syntonic. Refers to the acceptability of ideas or impulses to the ego. Opposite: *ego-alien.*

Electra complex. See *Oedipus complex.*

empathy. An intellectual understanding of the thoughts and feelings of another person; a form of identification.

empirical, empiricism. The approach which holds that the only source of knowledge is that which is objective or observable, *e.g.,* in psychology, behaviorism.

energy: See *libido.*

Eros. The "life instincts" or those instincts whose aims are sexual gratification and the perpetuation of life.

erotogenic zones. The surface areas of skin or mucous membranes which in response to friction create intense pleasurable feelings; especially the genitalia, lips, anus, and urethra.

etiology. Origin, history, or cause of a disorder.

fixation. Psychic energy remaining attached to objects or to a form of sexual pleasure normally dominant at an earlier stage of development.

free association. The "fundamental rule" of psychoanalytic treatment; the patient's spontaneous reporting of thoughts, with minimal rational or ethical control. Contrary to popular notions, requires hard work by the patient.

frustration. Environmental or psychological prevention of the gratification of an impulse.

functional. In psychiatry, the term *functional disorder* refers to symptomatology which is not caused by tissue destruction or by primary physiologic abnormality.

fundamental rule. See *free association.*

gratification. The fulfillment of an impulse and the pleasure which accompanies it.

hallucination. An apparent perception of an object for which no real (external) stimulus exists.

hypnosis. The induction of a trance-like state, characterized by the subject's high degree of responsiveness to suggestions.

hysteria. A psychoneurosis characterized by a physical symptom (*e.g.,* paralysis) without structural lesion. The term *conversion hysteria* signifies that psychic energy has been "converted" into a physical symptom which expresses the conflict symbolically.

id. That part of the personality which includes all of the unconscious instincts; the reservoir of psychic energy or libido, governed by the pleasure principle.

identification. A largely unconscious process in which an individual incorporates the real or imagined characteristics of another person and then thinks, feels, and acts in accordance with these characteristics.

impulse. In psychoanalysis, an instinct impelling the person to action.

infantile sexuality. See *psychosexual.*

instinct. Usual translation of Freud's term *Trieb*, which is more correctly rendered as drive; hence, an impulsion which is represented psychologically as a fantasy or wish. Gratification of the latter reduces the tension generated by an instinct.

interpretation. Applying the formulations of psychoanalytic theory to describe or explain a person's motivation or behavior; the major technique used in psychoanalytic therapy.

intrapsychic. Any function or process which is conceptualized as being in the psyche or mind.

introjection. Incorporation of the characteristics of a person into one's own ego structure with the corresponding tendency to identify with them.

latency period. The period of psychosexual development characterized by a relinquishment of sexual interests pertaining to the infantile phase in favor of activities and interests that take on the qualities of sublimations and reaction-formations. Occurs between the repression of the Oedipus complex and puberty, lasting approximately from age 6 to 13.

latent content. Those primary unconscious wishes which have activated a dream; discovered by analysis of the manifest content.

lay analyst. A person who has been trained in the psychoanalytic method of psychotherapy but who does not have a medical degree. (See also *psychoanalyst, psychotherapist.*)

libido. Psychic or instinctual energy; conceptualized as part of the id.

manic-depressive psychosis. A psychosis characterized by alternating periods of pathological excitement and periods of severe depression.

manifest content. The conscious waking memory of a dream. (See also *latent content.*)

masochism. A sexual perversion, characterized by the need to experience pain and humiliation in order to attain maximal erotic satisfaction. (See also *sadism.*)

narcissism. Love of self, complete self-centeredness; that stage of development in which the infant is ignorant of any source of pleasure other than himself.

neurology. The branch of medicine devoted to the study of the nervous system and its diseases.

neurosis. See *psychoneurosis.*

object. The aim of an instinct, usually a person.

obsession. Preoccupation with an idea which persists despite efforts to remove it from attention.

psychopath, psychopathic. See *sociopath, sociopathic.*

psychopathology. The study of mental disorders.

trance. See *hypnosis.*

obsessive-compulsive neurosis. A neurosis characterized by intruding thoughts and by repetitive impulses to perform certain acts (*e.g.,* hand-washing).

Oedipus complex. The erotic love, either conscious or unconscious, of male or female for either parent, accompanied by extreme jealousy of the other parent. In women, sometimes called *Electra complex.*

oral period. The first major period of psychosexual development, characterized by pleasurable sensations in the mucous membranes of the mouth through nursing, etc.

overdetermination. Refers to the multiple causes of a neurotic symptom or neurosis.

paralysis. See *hysteria.*

paranoid. An excessive unrealistic tendency to suspect others of hostile intentions and actions; prominently involves the defense mechanism of projection.

personality structure. All the conscious and unconscious aspects of the personality, including id, ego, and superego.

perversion. A term used to describe sexual practices which deviate from the normal or average, *e.g.,* homosexuality.

phallic period. A phase of psychosexual development preceding the Oedipal period in which the genitals are overvalued and in which relationships to other persons play a relatively minor role.

phobia. A neurotic anxiety reaction to a specific object or situation, as distinguished from generalized ("free-floating") anxiety.

physiology. The study of the functions of tissues and organs.

pleasure principle. A regulatory principle whose function is to reduce tension resulting from the instincts by immediate gratification, regardless of the consequences; characteristic of the instincts when not controlled by a mature ego operating under the reality principle. (See also *reality principle.*)

preconscious (noun). Those ideas which, though not conscious at the moment, can be readily made conscious by an effort of attention.

primary process. The laws which regulate events in the unconscious mind or id. The striving of the instincts for immediate discharge or satisfaction. (See also *secondary process.*)

projection. An ego-defense mechanism in which a threatening wish, trait, or thought is ascribed to someone else.

psychiatrist. A physician who specializes in the treatment of mental illness.

psychic. Relating to the psyche or mind.

psychoanalysis. (1) A theory of psychology, characterized by the importance placed upon unconscious mental processes. (2) A research method for investigating personality by means of free-association, dream-interpretation, etc. (3) A form of psychological treatment developed out of (1) and (2) above. (See also *psychotherapy*.)

psychoanalyst. A person trained in the theory and practice of psychoanalysis. (See also *psychotherapist*; *psychiatrist*; *lay therapist*.)

psychodynamics. The working of intrapsychic forces. (See also *intrapsychic*.)

psychogenic. Caused by the psyche or mind, *i.e.*, functional. (See also *functional*.)

psychology. The application of the scientific method to the study of behavior including perception, cognition, motivation, learning, etc. (See also *clinical psychology*.)

psychoneurosis (also neurosis). A psychological disorder often characterized by (1) sensory, motor, or visceral disturbances, (2) anxiety, (3) troublesome thoughts, (4) sleep disturbances, (5) sexual disturbances, (6) general inhibition. Reality contact remains similar to that of the rest of the community.

psychopath, psychopathic. See *sociopath, sociopathic*.

psychopathology. The study of mental disorders.

psychosexual. As used by Freud, encompasses all aspects of love and pleasure-seeking impulses.

psychosis. A serious mental disturbance, usually involving marked distortions of reality. Often but not always characterized by strange and bizarre feelings, beliefs, and behaviors. Roughly equivalent to the colloquial and legal term *insanity* which, however, has no longer scientific standing. (See also *manic-depressive psychosis; schizophrenia*.)

psychosomatic. Organic malfunction or disease in which psychological factors play a part.

psychotherapist. Generic term to describe a person trained in the theory and practice of psychotherapy. A psychoanalyst is a psychotherapist. (See also *psychoanalyst; psychiatrist; lay therapist*.)

psychotherapy. The systematic application of psychological principles and techniques for the purpose of changing a person's feelings, attitudes, and behavior in a more favorable direction. Psychoanalysis is a specialized form of psychotherapy. (See also *psychoanalysis*.)

reaction formation. A defense mechanism in which socially acceptable attitudes and behavior replace opposite unconscious impulses which are unacceptable to the ego. (See also *defense mechanism.*)

reality principle. A characteristic function of the ego designed to bring about a harmonious functioning of the total personality; typically involves delay of gratification. (See also *pleasure principle.*)

reality testing. A conscious ego function involving the discrimination of what has consensual validity in the person's environment as distinguished from fantasy.

regression. A return to an earlier or more primitive level of psychological functioning as a result of frustration or stress.

repression. An unconscious defense mechanism employed by the ego to exclude from conscious awareness wishes and impulses unacceptable to the ego. (See also *defense mechanism.*)

resistance. In psychoanalysis and other forms of psychotherapy, the patient's unconscious opposition to treatment.

sadism. A sexual perversion, characterized by the need to inflict pain and humiliation on others in order to experience maximal erotic satisfaction. Sadistic fantasies are usually accompanied by masochistic ones, and both are common. (See also *masochism.*)

schizophrenia. A group of psychoses often characterized by serious distortions of thinking and feeling, delusions, hallucinations, and bizarre behavior. (See also *psychosis.*)

secondary process. The laws which regulate events in the preconscious and conscious mind; the use of logic and reality-testing by the ego in regulating gratification of the instincts. (See also *primary process.*)

sexuality. See *psychosexuality.*

sociopath, sociopathic (also psychopath, psychopathic). A diagnostic term used to refer to a marked incapacity to restrain anti-social impulses accompanied by a normal awareness of the laws and mores and of the consequences of their violation. The psychopath tends to project the blame for his actions on others.

somatic. Pertaining to the body.

subconscious. A colloquial term for unconscious, lacking status in psychoanalytic theory.

sublimation. The process of gratifying an instinctual impulse in such a way as to conform to the demands of society.

superego. That part of the personality, largely unconscious, which threatens or imposes a sense of guilt. It is society's representative within the psyche; includes the conscience and the ego-ideal.

symbolization. The process by which the latent content of a dream is expressed in a substitutive or symbolic way, expressing in the manifest content something that is acceptable to the conscious mind of the dreamer.

syndrome. A set of symptoms indicative of a particular disease or disorder.

therapist. See *psychotherapist.*

therapy. See *psychotherapy.*

trance. See *hypnosis.*

transference. In psychoanalytic therapy, the projection of feelings, thoughts, and wishes onto the analyst, who has come to represent an object from the patient's past. The term *transference neurosis* refers to an intense form of the transference occurring typically in psychoanalytic treatment.

trauma. An intense excitation which cannot be mastered; may act as a primary or precipitating cause of a symptom.

Trieb. See *instinct.*

unconscious (adj.). Unaware or inaccessible to the conscious mind. (noun): A division of the mind including all unconscious mental phenomena and regulated by the primary process.

wish. The representation of an instinct in the mind. An impulse that strives for expression.

working through. Refers to the sustained effort required in psychotherapy to overcome conscious and unconscious resistances, thereby resolving or ameliorating neurotic patterns.

INDEX

Breinigsville, PA USA
07 December 2010
250763BV00001B/2/A